THE OPEN UNIVERSITY

Arts : A Third Level Course
Twentieth Century Poetry

Unit 27

ROBERT LOWELL

Prepared by Barry Chambers for the Course Team

The Open University Press

Cover   Illustration of a Chinook salmon

The Open University Press
Walton Hall, Milton Keynes
MK7 6AA

First published 1976

Designed by the Media Development Group of the Open University.

Printed in Great Britain by
EYRE AND SPOTTISWOODE LIMITED
AT GROSVENOR PRESS PORTSMOUTH

ISBN 0 335 05118 9

This text forms part of an Open University course. The complete list of units in the course appears at the end of this text.

For general availability of supporting material referred to in this text, please write to the Director of Marketing, The Open University, P.O. Box 81, Walton Hall, Milton Keynes, MK7 6AT.

Further information on Open University courses may be obtained from the Admissions Office, The Open University, P.O. Box 48, Walton Hall, Milton Keynes MK7 6AB.

1.1

CONTENTS UNIT 27

INTRODUCTION TO UNITS 27–32

With this unit on Robert Lowell's poetry, we begin the final section of the course, and as you may recall from *A Guide to the Course*, there is a change both of emphasis and approach.

In terms of literary history we have now brought our survey up to about 1950. By that date, the poets you have been studying so far had either completed their major achievement, or if they were still in mid-career, had already made their individual impact. Poets who achieved reputation during the 1950s were influenced by them; they were reacting against the influence of, not only Eliot and Yeats and Hardy (Pound rather less so), but also of Auden whose voice had commanded the thirties, and of Dylan Thomas who was very influential in the forties. You should now be in a position to enter into the situation of the young writers of the period 1950–70, for whom the work of these poets, together with that of William Empson (critic and poet), and F. R. Leavis, constituted a major part of the inherited literary culture. One of our reasons for bringing the course more or less up to the present day was to make this kind of point. A living literary tradition is always such a matrix of influences, from the recent past, some strengthening, some fading, both critically received and, on occasion, eluded.

But there is also a difficulty about including contemporary poetry. How does one select amongst the many poets who deserve attention? We may be too near them to make a sensible judgement. The best solution would have been a representative anthology of recent writing, but none was available when we planned the course. The selection made for Units 27–32 has, no doubt, its arbitrary aspect, though we feel no hesitation about its potential interest. It is, perhaps, best considered *as* an anthology, made up of preliminary critical essays and a selection of poems intended to introduce you to intrinsically rewarding poetry from the last twenty or so years.

Three criteria guided us in our choice. One was to register an important new fact about post-war British poetry, the impact on it of American poetry. This aspect is represented by the poetry of Robert Lowell (Unit 27) and of Sylvia Plath (Unit 29), though not too much weight should be placed on 'represented' since the interaction between the two literary cultures is now extensive and continuing. Second, we wanted to include poets of an earlier generation, relatively untouched by the main 'Modernist' influences, whose work perhaps for that reason attracted a new attention in recent decades. These are Robert Graves and John Betjeman, discussed in Unit 30. Thirdly, and most importantly, we have included a group of poets who began to publish in the 1950s, who represent the important developments from, or against, the 'Modernist' tradition: Philip Larkin (Unit 28), Ted Hughes (Unit 29), Donald Davie, Charles Tomlinson and Geoffrey Hill (Unit 31).

There remains Unit 32, which reflects two trends. One is the importance to the modern reader of poetry-in-translation, a theme already touched on earlier in the course, and here represented by the work of Zbigniew Herbert (Polish), Miroslav Holub (Czechoslovak), and Vasko Popa (Yugoslavian). The other is the development of another attempt (Georgianism and Thirties poetry are earlier cases) to seek a wider audience for poetry than the usual small minority of the reading public. This effort took the form of a poetry-in-performance, sometimes to music, more often at poetry readings to large audiences. Poetry of this kind has been attacked for its superficiality, its fashionable trendiness of sentiment. But as a recent survey of the period points out:

> It remains the case that most poets of great interest are 'difficult', even if,
> like Dylan Thomas or Carlos Williams, their surface charm disguises it.

Great verse is still not obviously suitable for the mass audience. If the climate inhabited by poetry in Britain in 1970 seemed more hopeful than any experienced earlier in the century, this was perhaps a result of the genuine success of mass education; the complex and hermetic lyrics of Bob Dylan were readily accepted by a great part of a whole generation as part of their culture (as distinct from their 'serious' reading or their academic culture), and this was surely an advance from the days of Newbolt.[1]

In reading this group of units, keep in mind the intended resemblance to an anthology, and follow your own tastes and enthusiasms. You may sometimes find that the number of poems included by each unit author is too small to satisfy, and decide to read more widely. But there should be enough in each selection for the basis of a TMA, provided you read the poems attentively. In each unit you will also find suggestions for assignment topics. *Please treat these only as a guide.* If you prefer to work out your own, that is greatly to be encouraged – though remember to consult your tutor to make sure you do not embark on something too time-consuming. As to further critical reading, unit authors provide advice about this, but in general you should keep to short introductory books (those in the series published by Oliver and Boyd, for example), and put your main energy into reading more poems. That is one of the beauties of looking at contemporary writing. There is no critical consensus to worry about. You are on your own, a contemporary reader, responding in your own terms.

[1]Angus Calder 'British Poetry and Its Audience 1914–70' in *Literature and Western Civilization* (1976) (ed David Daiches and Anthony Thorlby) Aldus Books.

ROBERT LOWELL

1 INTRODUCTION

AN OUTLINE OF LOWELL'S POETIC VOLUMES

1.1 Robert Lowell was born in Boston, Massachusetts, on 1 March 1917. His first volume of poetry was published in 1944. An English edition did not appear until 1950 when Faber brought out *Poems 1938–49*. That volume was in fact a collection of poems from three earlier American publications. It included seven poems from *Land of Unlikeness* (1944), all the poems from *Lord Weary's Castle* (1946), and all but the title poem from *The Mills of the Kavanaughs* (1951). This volume, which formed the basis for Lowell's international reputation, remains the most convenient source for a representative collection of works from his first poetic phase.

1.2 Lowell's next volume, *Life Studies*, was published in 1959. It seems to mark a turning-point in his poetic career because in this work Lowell appears to have moved towards an intense personal involvement with his poetry. Since he seemed to be producing poetry out of his own experiences, out of his sufferings and psychological problems, the critics coined the term 'confessional' to describe the resulting poetry.

1.3 That rather dismissive epithet clung to Lowell despite the fact that his next volume of poetry consisted of very free adaptations of certain non-English poets, including Baudelaire, Rimbaud, Rilke and Pasternak: that is to say that Lowell's own voice and experiences were displaced by those of the other poets. These adaptations were published under the title *Imitations* and appeared in 1961.[1]

1.4 His next volume of poetry was *For the Union Dead*, published in 1964. That too would seem to merit a term other than 'confessional' if only because it is geographically, historically and sociologically speaking, quite far-ranging. However, *Near the Ocean* (1967), the next book of poems, does seem to be a return to the poetry of self-revelation through autobiographical details. This also seems to be the case with *Notebook, 1967–8* which appeared in 1969.

1.5 Lowell's last two collections of poetry are *For Lizzie and Harriet* (1973) and *The Dolphin* (1973). These works, together with *History* (1973) are a continuation of the self-revelatory techniques; in fact, of these last three publications, only *The Dolphin* is substantially new, the other two are mainly re-workings and re-orderings of earlier material.

1.6 These are the main and easily accessible volumes of Lowell's poetry which you should look for if you wish to read more of Lowell than I have space to print in this unit. They are all published by Faber, as is a very useful paperback edition of *Selected Poems* which prints eight early poems from *Poems 1938–49*, fifteen from *Life Studies* and seven from *For the Union Dead*. At the end of the unit I include a short biographical note. I also give some suggestions for further reading and work.

SUGGESTED POINTERS TOWARDS READING LOWELL'S POETRY

1.7 Before I begin my study of Lowell's poetry I would like to suggest one or two pointers which might help you on your way towards a full appreciation of his qualities. In the first place I want to emphasize that, although he has been for some time now a resident in England, Lowell is essentially an American poet. I am not now thinking

---

[1]You will recall that Lowell's view of translation is discussed in Unit 12, *Poetry in Translation*.

of the obvious differences observable on the level of American rather than English terminology, but, more importantly, of something rather less easy to isolate. English readers sometimes find it difficult to understand what Henry James meant when he claimed that it was 'a complex fate, being an American', mainly, I think, because the question of personal and national definition is not so acute if one lives in a country which is more than two hundred years old. The great experiment of creating a new nation out of the enormous 'melting pot' formed by immigrants from the whole world has been in operation for a relatively short period. Michel de Crèvecoeur in his *Letters from an American Farmer* (1782, 1783) asked a question which still has relevance: 'What then is the American, this new man?' Americans have been trying to show themselves, and the world, the answer ever since.

1.8   A characteristic problem for the American, then, is the one which concerns a definition of self. That, inevitably, involves the wider perspective of relationship with the nation. This leads to a special concern with the identity of the nation on all levels – historical, political, social – in a way which Europeans rarely share.

1.9   One obvious manifestation of a need to define oneself as American is an examination of one's family history in its contributions towards the development of the country. In Lowell's case, descended as he is from two illustrious families (who can count in their ranks a Pilgrim Father who arrived on the *Mayflower*, a Governor of Plymouth Colony, a famous New Hampshire frontiersman who was a general in the Revolutionary War, teachers, clergymen, naval officers, a Harvard professor and distinguished poet . . .) the need to look backwards might seem to be all the more pressing. In fact, his awareness of his place in the history of his family and country is an obvious characteristic of Lowell's early poetry in the sense that many of the poems deal with specific concerns of his ancestry, and notably his New England heritage. In his early poems you will see Lowell exploring his religious background. It was clearly an important means whereby he could come to terms with the past. As he has put it in a later poem: 'I am learning to live in history.'

1.10   One characteristic of Lowell's examination of the past is a qualified optimism about the future. As you read further in his work I would like you to pay particular attention to the tone which I find remarkably consistent. Although I don't want to attempt to spell out a philosophy for Lowell, I do think that he has reached a position rather like that expressed by Matthew Arnold's Empedocles, who says 'Make us not fly to dreams, but moderate desire.' (Penguin Poets, *Matthew Arnold*, p 46.) Indeed, Arnold's description of the poet who has ceased to nurse 'extravagant hope' as having a 'sad lucidity of soul' ('Resignation', *Matthew Arnold*, p 168) seems particularly well-suited to Robert Lowell's poetic voice. Lowell seems to have reached this position by an awareness of the dangers of idealisms. He is well aware that idealism has a way of turning sour and becoming tyranny. His examination of various characters in his own as well as his nation's history illustrates this. Do note though that this awareness of the discrepancy between noble ideals and their extension in actuality does not produce despair but a 'sad lucidity'. This, you might feel, is not a bad basis for a *modus vivendi*.

1.11   Although I am not going to attempt here to summarize Lowell's development in terms of poetic technique, I would like to point out one important characteristic. Look at the following lines

> Tamed by *Miltown*, we lie on Mother's bed;
> the rising sun in war paint dyes us red;
> in broad daylight her gilded bed-posts shine,
> abandoned, almost Dionysian.
> At last the trees are green on Marlborough Street,
> blossoms on our magnolia ignite
> the morning with their murderous five days' white.

This is the opening of the poem 'Man and Wife' from *Life Studies*.[2] A good deal of its force comes from the fact that here Lowell is deliberately echoing the opening lines of Book II of Milton's *Paradise Lost*.

High on a throne of royal state, which far
Outshone the wealth of Ormus and of Ind,
Or where the gorgeous East with richest hand
Showers on her kings barbaric pearl and gold,
Satan exalted sat, by merit rais'd
To that bad eminence; and from despair
Thus high uplifted beyond hope, aspires
Beyond thus high, insatiate to pursue
Vain war with Heav'n . . .

(*Paradise Lost* Book II, lines 1–9.)

Figure 1   Robert Lowell (Camera Press (G/M) London)

More than that, *Miltown* is a well known tranquillizer, thus, the word becomes a significant pun. However, what I want to point out here is the way in which domestic reality is quite vividly presented in terms which suggest another epic, if doomed, opulence. The Lowells' contemporary domesticity, which is a peace assisted by the tranquillizing effect of Miltown/Milton, is not destroyed by comparison with Milton's epic. The present reality which substitutes the marriage bed (which is not even theirs!) for Satan's splendid throne is not belittled by the contrast: it is more nearly the reverse of that because the total effect of the poem is to suggest that modern domesticity could be the grounds for a new epic poetry.

[2]These lines are read on band 3 side 1 of record 1, *Rhythms of Poetry*, ou21.

1.12 Lowell makes frequent use of allusion and that fact plus the frequent references to somewhat esoteric American detail has resulted in some fairly heavy footnoting by me in the poems printed in this unit. Don't be discouraged or dismayed by the wealth of detail. I believe that the poems work on several levels and the most important one for your own first readings is probably on the level of the imagery. If you have followed the poetic technique of *Four Quartets* in the way that images echo and re-echo through the mind carrying an essentially ineffable 'message', then you will be well on your way to appreciating Lowell. His poetry contains imagery of vivid physical detail, rooted in our real world, which somehow develops its own story-line so that you need not know all the wealth of allusion which might be present. It is with this belief in mind that I ask you to read the following poems paying more attention to the form than the content. What I mean by that is simply that I think it will be a mistake if you try to produce a paraphrasable 'message' for each poem. My notes on the first four poems go as far as I would wish in that direction. My first concern here is for you to gain some understanding of Lowell's poetic ways so that you can follow up and read much more of the work of this highly praised contemporary poet on your own.

1.13 In Section 3 I offer more detailed discussion of some longer poems and in Section 4 I suggest aspects of the cultural background which might help you place Lowell in perspective.

2 'PLOTTED' 'OUTLOOK' 'THE FIRST SUNDAY IN LENT' 'GRANDPARENTS'

Plotted

Planes arc like arrows through the highest sky,
ducks V the ducklings across a puckered pond;
Providence turns animals to things.
I roam from bookstore to bookstore browsing books,
I too maneuvered on a guiding string
as I execute my written plot.
I feel how Hamlet, stuck with the Revenge Play
his father wrote him, went scatological
under this clotted London sky.
Catlike on a paper parapet,
he declaimed the words his prompter fed him,
knowing convention called him forth to murder,
loss of free will and licence of the stage.
Death's not an event in life, it's not lived through.

(*The Dolphin*, p 49.)

Outlook

On my rainy outlook, the great shade is up,
my window, five feet wide, is raised a foot,
most of the view is blanked by brick and windows.
Domestic gusts of noonday Sunday cooking;
black snow grills on the fire-escape's blacker iron,
like the coal that touched Isaiah's unclean tongue . . .[3]

[3]Isaiah 6: 5–7.

10

I hear dead sounds ascending, the fertile stench
of horsedroppings from the war-year of my birth.
Since our '17, how many millions gone –[4]
this same street, West Sixty-Seven, was here,
and this same building, the last gasp of true,
Nineteenth Century Capitalistic Gothic –
horsedroppings and drippings . . . hear it, hear the clopping
hundreds of horses unstopping . . . each hauls a coffin.

(Originally from *Notebook*, revised and included in *History*, p 206.)

The First Sunday in Lent

I

'In the Attic'

The crooked family chestnut sighs, for March,
Time's fool, is storming up and down the town;
The gray snow squelches and the well-born stamp
From sermons in a scolded, sober mob
That wears away the Sabbath with a frown,
A world below my window. What will clamp
The week-kneed roots together when the damp
Aches like a conscience, and they grope to rob
The hero under his triumphal arch?

This is the fifth floor attic where I hid
My stolen agates and the cannister
Preserved from Bunker Hill[5] – feathers and guns,
Matchlock and flintlock and percussion-cap;
Gettysburg etched upon the cylinder
Of Father's Colt. A Luger of a Hun,
Once blue as Satan, breaks Napoleon,
My china pitcher. Cartridge boxes trap
A chipmunk on the sabre where they slid.[6]

On Troy's last day, alas, the populous
Shrines held carnival, and girls and boys
Flung garlands to the wooden horse; so we
Burrow into the lion's mouth to die.
Lord, from the lust and dust thy will destroys
Raise an unblemished Adam who will see
The limbs of the tormented chestnut tree
Tingle, and hear the March-winds lift and cry:
'The Lord of Hosts will overshadow us.'

[4]Lowell was born 1 March 1917, the year America entered the First World War.
[5]17 June 1775. The scene of a bloody clash between the British and the rebels on the outskirts of
Boston. Both sides lost substantial numbers of men and materials.
[6]A difficult few lines. Here is an apparent reference to personal details relating to actual material from
the attic of Lowell's youth. The luger must be a souvenir of either the First or Second World War.
It was a German hand-gun, presumably metallic blue/grey in colour. It seems to have fallen against
and broken a china jug called Napoleon by the young Lowell. Perhaps it had a picture of Napoleon
as decoration? The chipmunk was presumably a stuffed one – or perhaps even a picture – but it has
been pushed along a sabre by some cartridge boxes due to haphazard movements as more junk is put
in the attic. Notice particularly how Lowell uses this detail to telescope materials from various wars.

II

'The Ferris Wheel'[7]

This world, this ferris wheel, is tired and strains
Its townsman's humorous and bulging eye,
As he ascends and lurches from his seat
And dangles by a shoe-string overhead
To tell the racing world that it must die.
Who can remember what his father said?
The little wheel is turning on the great
In the white water of Christ's blood. The red
Eagle of Ares[8] swings along the lanes,

Of camp-stools where the many watch the sky:
The townsman hangs, the eagle swings. It stoops
And lifts the ferris wheel into the tent
Pitched for the devil. But the man works loose,
He drags and zigzags through the circus hoops,
And lion-taming Satan bows and loops
His cracking tail into a hangman's noose;
He is the only happy man in Lent.
He laughs into my face until I cry.

(*Poems 1939–1949*, pp 25–6.)

Grandparents

They're altogether otherworldly now,
those adults champing for their ritual Friday spin
to pharmacist and five-and-ten[9] in Brockton.
Back in my throw-away and shaggy span
of adolescence, Grandpa still waves his stick
like a policeman;
Grandmother, like a Mohammedan, still wears her thick
lavender mourning and touring veil,
the Pierce Arrow[10] clears its throat in a horse-stall.
Then the dry road dust rises to whiten
the fatigued elm leaves –
the nineteenth century, tired of children, is gone.
They're all gone into a world of light;[11] the farm's my own.

The farm's my own!
Back there alone,
I keep indoors, and spoil another season.
I hear the rattley little country gramophone
racking its five foot horn:
'O summer Time!'

---

[7]The 'Big Wheel' of the fairground which carries passengers in cars slung from supports within its periphery. So called after its American inventor, G. W. G. Ferris.
[8]This is rather puzzling because Ares was a Greek not a Roman god and the eagle was the symbol of Jupiter, not Mars. Lowell seems to have telescoped the references.
[9]A store which specializes in inexpensive items; i.e. goods for a nickel (five cents) or a dime (ten cents).
[10]An early American motor car.
[11]The title and first line of a poem by Henry Vaughan (1622–95). See *Oxford Book of Seventeenth-Century Verse*, pp 781–2.

Even at noon here the formidable
Ancien Régime still keeps nature at a distance. Five
green shaded light bulbs spider the billiards-table,
no field is greener than its cloth,
where Grandpa, dipping sugar for us both,
once spilled his demitasse.
His favourite ball, the number three,
still hides the coffee stain.

Never again
to walk there, chalk our cues,
insist on shooting for us both.
Grandpa! Have me, hold me, cherish me!
Tears smut my fingers. There
half my life-lease later,
I hold an *Illustrated London News*,
disloyal still,
I doodle handlebar
moustaches on the last Russian Czar.

(*Life Studies*, p 82.)

PLOTTED

2.1 It would be stretching things a bit if we were to describe this poem as a sonnet. Although it has fourteen lines, it is unrhymed and the lines are not regularly iambic or decasyllabic. It does, however, have an informal pattern which helps in the expression of whatever it is Lowell is saying.

2.2 Like the Italian sonnet (see *A Guide to the Course*) this poem is in two parts. Unlike the Italian sonnet, the first part consists of six lines (the sestet) followed by eight lines (the octave). The first part is descriptive and the second reflective. This arrangement associates two images of arrow-like movement with the idea of a human being following some predetermined course. In the octave, that idea is expanded by the reference to Hamlet's predicament. However, the use of the Hamlet image in this setting deepens the notion of predetermined behaviour mainly because of the way Lowell places himself within the framework of the poem. The poetic 'I' is related to Hamlet who was 'stuck with the Revenge Play/his father wrote him'. This would seem to suggest that the past has an overpowering influence upon the present, but notice that Lowell also implies Hamlet's awareness of his situation. The effect is to convey the impression that Hamlet was capable of independent thought despite the fact that he exists only as a character within a play. In reaction to being 'stuck' within the framework of the Revenge Play provided by his father, he 'went scatological'. Despite having to declaim his set speeches, he is presented as 'knowing convention called him forth'.

2.3 This kind of awareness certainly increases the complexity when related to the poetic 'I' because the act of writing is analogous to Hamlet's words and actions. Look particularly at the line 'as I execute my written plot'. The play on the word 'execute' is intriguing. It is first of all to be seen in the situation in which Hamlet was called upon to act out his father's revenge. In order to carry out (i.e. 'execute') his father's wish, he had to put to death (i.e. 'execute' in the judicial sense of following a sentence) his uncle.[12] In Lowell's poem, the 'I' creates the thought in a literary form, that is to

---

[12]There is also the notion of the word as indicative of an executor who carries out the wishes of the deceased in matters of estate.

13

say he 'executes' it, but in so doing his sense of awareness destroys ('executes') 'the written plot'. In that way, the writing of poetry for the 'I' of this poem is the equivalent of Hamlet going 'scatological'. 'Scatological' is the adjectival form of the noun 'scatology' which is that branch of medical science which diagnoses disease by examination of excrement. As an image for Hamlet's predicament it indicates the poet's awareness of the tragi-comic element: as an image for his own situation it shows a self-deprecating, wry humour. This tone is aided by the almost conversational metrical form Lowell uses. In addition, the comparatively few run-on endings of the lines – often emphasized by the punctuation – and the lack of rhyme, give the impression of a series of statements which at first sight seem rather disconnected. However, they are not only linked by the development of the images; the technical devices of alliteration and assonance indicate a kinship between the ducks, the 'I' and Hamlet.

> ducks V the ducklings across a puckered pond . . .
> I roam from bookstore to bookstore browsing books . . .
> Catlike on a paper parapet . . .

Also, quite unobtrusively, near-rhymes echo within the poem – 'things'/'string', 'plot'/'clotted'.

2.4   The total effect is to give the impression of a fairly casual reflection upon a real-life observation. The fact that it is not at all casual but carefully 'plotted' is itself a fine irony and draws our attention to the personality of the 'I' of the poem. My impression of him is that he is a highly intelligent skilled craftsman with a sense of humour which takes as its base an awareness of the individual's limited scope for independent manoeuvring. Do you agree? Did you find anything like this in the next poem?

OUTLOOK

2.5   Once again, there is the fourteen-line, unrhymed poem but here there is greater regularity in the line length and, depending upon the stress pattern you might give it, it is nearer to a blank verse line. However, this too avoids the regular iambic rise and fall, again giving the impression of a conversational reflection from a poet whose attitude to his subject matter is discernible from his tone of voice as well as from direct statement.

2.6   There is a similar sestet/octave division as in 'Plotted', in that the first six lines deal with the observed scene, but in this poem the simile from Isaiah in the sixth line makes the division into two parts less pronounced than in the first poem.

2.7   There might be superficial similarities on the level of the forms of the two poems but there is a fundamental difference in the viewpoints expressed. In 'Plotted' the 'I' of the poem found a way of coming to terms with a pre-plotted existence; this involved an awareness of the tragi-comic nature of the predicament. In 'Outlook' the viewpoint is much more sombre with no hint of any kind of humour. There is much less subtlety in the presentation of the poem's main theme. The bleak, hemmed in 'rainy outlook' from the poet's home is an easily appreciated analogue for a spiritual state. The explicit reference is to the millions dead in this century since 1917, the year of the poet's birth. The connection between the sestet and octave – the observed detail from life and the reflection upon it – is the dripping from rain and melting snow, via the 'dead sounds' and 'horsedroppings'. This leads to the last two lines of the poem which, by virtue of the near rhyme 'clopping'/'coffin', is almost a couplet which is the way the traditional English sonnet ended.

2.8 I would take this last point about poetic form and put it beside something else in the sestet as indicative of something characteristic of Lowell. I am referring to the way in which, in the act of making the poem, Lowell is at once participator and interpreter. In 'Plotted' there is the ironic juxtaposition of the poetic 'I' and Hamlet, culminating in the ambiguities of 'execute'; in 'Outlook' there is the image of Isaiah whose unclean lips are purged by one of the seraphim that he might go and be God's messenger. Here there is the clear implication of the poem's role as a potential agent of social change. Indeed, in the concentration upon the numbers dead since 1917 – 'how many million gone' there is a telescoping of Isaiah's 'how long?' and God's answer: 'Until cities be waste without inhabitants, and houses without man, and the land become utterly waste.' (Isaiah 7: 11.) This kind of association is important because it shows how Lowell intends the image of 'horsedropping' described as having a 'fertile stench'. The 'millions gone' would seem to be a necessary condition in the Isaiah sense for the eventual fertilization for the 'new stock'. This is the gloomy vision, the 'rainy outlook' upon which the shade has been opened. The fact that Lowell recognizes this outlook as bringing inevitable misery for millions of individuals is apparent in the pointless monotony of 'horsedroppings and drippings'. It is also very clear from the last line of 'Plotted', because, for the 'millions gone' there is nothing more: death is 'not an event in life, it's not lived through'.

2.9 This kind of viewpoint is not despairing or bitter; it is resigned. The same base-line of only moderate expectation – to put it at its highest – is also apparent in Lowell's image for the snow on the black iron on the fire-escape, that is, Isaiah's burning coal. Like the Hamlet/poet link, the Isaiah/poet link says very little for the effectiveness of the poem as an agent of change. The best it might be thought to do would be to bring about an awareness of how things really are. In this connection you might like to know that in discussion with Gabriel Pearson from which television programme 13 was made Lowell said, 'all literature . . . can give awareness of reality. That may do no good, maybe it's not a very good thing to have an awareness of reality, but we assume it is, that should be the artist's act of faith.' You might like to consider this attitude to reality in relation to Eliot's as seen, for example, in *Four Quartets*. In addition, perhaps you were aware of the way in which Lowell works from clearly evoked images of reality which are quite startling in their physical presence. For instance, 'horsedroppings and drippings' . . . 'clopping hundreds of horses un-stopping'.

THE FIRST SUNDAY IN LENT

2.10 Perhaps the first thing to be noticed about this poem is its regularity. Its two parts consist of stanzas made up of nine lines of blank verse rhyming *abcdbccda* except in the two stanzas of part two where there is variety in the rhymes of lines 6, 7 and 8. Yet, despite this tight metrical and rhyme form Lowell still achieves a conversational tone. Note particularly the second stanza in part one where the run-on lines break up any tendency to linger on the rhyme word at the end of a line.

2.11 What is the underlying notion of reality in this work? Is it anything like that which informs the other two poems? And is there any similarity of techniques in the presentation of the viewpoint?

2.12 To take the last point first, it does seem that Lowell is here using the method of starting from observed human detail of the here and now in order to move to a reflection about the human predicament generally. In this we have the pattern of the two sonnets discussed above. In the case of 'The First Sunday in Lent', if we consider the two parts as one, we can see how the two opening stanzas are mainly descriptive and the two closing stanzas reflective in the sense that they place man in an historical and religious context which suggests the contemporaneity of the past. Between these stanzas comes a linking stanza which unites the two parts in the same way as did the Hamlet and Isaiah images in joining sestet and octave.

Figure 2 Illustration from the title page of Lord Weary's Castle, 1946, with drawing of Cain killing Abel by Francis Parker (Reproduced by courtesy of the publishers Harcourt Brace Jovanovich)

2.13 This third stanza of part one takes us through an invocation to the Lord to 'Raise an unblemished Adam' back to the first stanza and the chestnut tree as it is being moved by the March winds. In the first stanza the tree is described as sighing in the winds of March and this complements the mood of the townspeople as they return home 'a scolded, sober mob'. Their stamping home and March's 'storming up and down' produce the chestnut's sigh. In the third stanza the vision which is prayed for the 'unblemished Adam' is one which will see 'The limbs of the tormented chestnut tree/ *Tingle*,' presumably with returning life. That is to say, the ability to see beyond the immediate present to the underlying cycle of death and rebirth. This, of course, is presented in the religious context. The reminder of the Trojan mistake over the wooden horse, following as it does the catalogue of the material possessions heaped in the attic, serves to imply a similar mistake which, in fact, hastens our end. Look again at the details of those possessions and see how they infer a history of wartime violence.

2.14 The cyclical notion of death and rebirth is given in its most obvious form in the second part called 'The Ferris Wheel'. Here the difficulty at first is following what appears to be a confusion of images. Lowell makes the basic image of the fairground

16

ferris wheel stand as an analogue for the earth. This releases many associations in our minds but central to this image is the special torment of one who is precariously caught in the machinery of the wheel. He

> . . . dangles by a shoe-string overhead
> To tell the racing world that it must die.

This, suggests Lowell, is Christ's message to the world and his personal involvement was needed because: 'Who can remember what his father said?' Lowell adds to this fairground image the picture of the Roman legions with their eagle emblem of Ares, the god of war. It is this eagle which carries Christ and the wheel into the devil's world. From this point the image of Satan as Ringmaster tormenting Christ until he escapes takes over and in the implication of the spectacle being watched as entertainment we have an attitude which might remind you of the Kafka short story *In the Gallery*.

2.15 Do not worry too much about sorting out all the details of Lowell's thought in this particular instance. At this point all I want to establish is the vision of reality upon which the poem is based, and to suggest some of the ways in which Lowell presents it. This poem first appeared in *Lord Weary's Castle* (1946), Lowell's second volume of poetry. At the time of writing he was clearly interpreting life from the religious viewpoint which his entry into the Roman Catholic Church in 1940 gave him. The title of the collection itself derives from a ballad which is based upon man's ingratitude for Christ's sacrifice. With that starting point it complements the inspiration for the first volume, *Land of Unlikeness* (1944). For that collection Lowell recalled St Bernard's words about man having lost his understanding of his soul's likeness to God. The vision of contemporary society expressed in these volumes is, therefore, rather like Eliot's in that it is seen as a waste land where man has lost his purpose because he has lost sight of God.

GRANDPARENTS

2.16 This poem appeared in *Life Studies* in 1959. After 'The First Sunday in Lent', this poem will probably strike you as being very free in form and personal in content. There is no regular metre or rhyme; neither is there a hint of a religious interpretation. The poem seems to be wholly concerned with Lowell's feelings about his grandparents, particularly in regard to their home, the farm which he now owns.

2.17 The poem opens in an amusing way because it capitalizes upon our own notions of grandparents as belonging to another era, another world. Now Lowell's grandparents are dead they are '*altogether* otherworldly now'. Here the humour is without criticism as is the case also in the descriptions of them 'champing' to begin a part of their weekly routine of shopping. Although there might be grounds for using them as a symbol of aimlessness – a dedication to materialism say – in this poem that interpretation is not present. Lowell's concern with them is to express his own attitude to the past. Like D. H. Lawrence in 'Piano' he 'weeps like a child for the past' but, unlike Lawrence, Lowell ends his poem on a basically humorous note. He uses an experience familiar to us all from childhood. Despite the adult tendency to sentimentality, instinctively, like a child, he doodles upon a magazine. He refers to this as being 'disloyal still'. This sketches in the vague notions, familiar to us since childhood, of falling short of adult standards. The doodling destroys the sentiment but is a realistic version of the way things really are.

2.18 Although ostensibly about a personal situation, the poem so uses familiar images that it transcends the private experience. It becomes a poem about coming to terms with one's own life against the background of obvious mutability. There is a sense in which we all inherit the farm but perhaps we are not all able to cauterise the emotion and

> . . . doodle handlebar
> moustaches on the last Russian Czar.

Although the vision of reality is not the same, this method of using images which echo in the mind might remind you of the way in which Eliot uses the images of *Alice in Wonderland*, and the Chinese jar in 'Burnt Norton'.

2.19 The four poems discussed above should give you some indication of the scope and characteristics of Robert Lowell's poetry. He is clearly a poet concerned with serious metaphysical issues concerning man in the universe. He is, just as clearly, an accomplished technician. In Section 3 I wish to illustrate, with more detail, the ways in which some of the important issues have been treated in the creation of some of his most celebrated poems.

3 'IN MEMORY OF ARTHUR WINSLOW' 'AFTER THE SURPRISING CONVERSIONS' 'MEMORIES OF WEST STREET AND LEPKE' 'FOR THE UNION DEAD' 'WAKING EARLY SUNDAY MORNING'

3.1 Puritan New England, and especially Boston, figure prominently in the cultural history of America. From the early seventeenth-century settlements in the Calvinistic Massachusetts Bay Colony to the nineteenth-century Transcendentalists, this area had supplied leaders of spiritual, political and cultural thought. For two hundred years this area had given the basis of a class system to the country. Leading families traced their ancestry back to *Mayflower* pioneers who played decisive parts the life of the nation. In Boston, the fame of two particular families is enshrined in an old rhyme:

> And this is good old Boston,
> The home of the bean and the cod,
> Where the Lowells talk only to Cabots,
> And Cabots talk only to God.

Robert Lowell was born into the second great family of Boston but in 1917 the traditional notions of aristocracy no longer had the force of the past. However, it is a fact that Lowell's mother was descended from Edward Winslow, a Pilgrim Father, whose son became Governor of the Plymouth Colony. This illustrious ancestry is further enhanced by a hero of the Revolutionary War, General John Stark. Both families, the Winslows and the Starks, are referred to in the next poem I wish to discuss. The Arthur Winslow of the poem's title is Lowell's grandfather – his mother's father. This poem was first collected in *Lord Weary's Castle* (1946) and is included in *Poems 1938–1949* (1950).

3.2 ■ In your first reading of this poem try to relate it to some of the things you have already noticed about Lowell's poetic technique. You might especially consider the way he refers to the present in terms of the past. What effect does this have?

In Memory of Arthur Winslow[13]

I

'Death from Cancer'

This Easter, Arthur Winslow, less than dead,
Your people set you up in Phillips' House
To settle off your wrestling with the crab —[14]
The claws drop flesh upon your yachting blouse
Until longshoreman Charon[15] come and stab
Through your adjusted bed
And crush the crab. On Boston Basin, shells[16]
Hit water by the Union Boat Club wharf:
You ponder why the coxes'[17] squeakings dwarf
The *resurrexit dominus*[18] of all the bells.

Grandfather Winslow, look, the swanboats[19] coast
That island in the Public Gardens, where
The bread-stuffed ducks are brooding, where with tub[20]
And strainer the mid-Sunday Irish scare
The sun-struck shallows for the dusky chub
This Easter, and the ghost
Of risen Jesus walks the waves to run[21]
Arthur upon a trumpeting black swan
Beyond Charles River to the Acheron[22]
Where the wide waters and their voyager are one.

II

'Dunbarton'

The stones are yellow and the grass is gray
Past Concord by the rotten lake and hill
Where crutch and trumpet meet the limousine
And half-forgotten Starks and Winslows fill
The granite plot and the dwarf pines are green
From watching for the day
When the great year of the little yeoman[23] come
Bringing its landed Promise[24] and the faith
That made the Pilgrim Makers take a lathe
And point their wooden steeples lest the Word be dumb.

[13]Arthur Winslow – Lowell's grandfather, his mother's father – was a Boston businessman descended from the Stark family of Dunbarton, New Hampshire as well as the Winslows of Massachusetts.
[14]Crab: A reference to cancer since that is the Latin word for crab.
[15]Charon: In Greek mythology Charon is the ferryman who carries the souls of the dead across the river Styx.
[16]On Boston Basin, shells: A reference to the racing shells, i.e. lightweight rowing boats, which are using the water in the Boston Basin.
[17]Coxes: These are the lightweight steersmen, coxwains, of the boats.
[18]*Resurrexit dominus*: The bells are pealing the Easter message of 'The Lord is risen.'
[19]Swanboats: This is probably a periphrasis for 'swans'. I know of no boat with this name.
[20]Tub and strainer: A reference to a rudimentary net with which the visitors to the Public Gardens would attempt to catch 'chub' a species of carp. The tub is the small bucket-like container which would hold the catch.
[21]To run/Arthur: A reference to Jesus walking on the water. Matthew 14: 25.
[22]Acheron: Here Lowell links the Charles River of Boston with the river in Hades in Greek mythology.
[23]Little Yeoman: A reference to colonial times. In New England at that time the majority of the settlers were freeholders of land.
[24]Its landed Promise: A reference to the promised land which awaited those who were 'saved' on the Day of Judgement, but there is also a clear play on the notion of land from the reference to the 'little yeoman'.

O fearful witnesses, your day is done:
The minister from Boston waves your shades,
Like children, out of sight and out of mind.
The first selectman of Dunbarton spreads
Wreaths of New Hampshire pine cones on the lined
Casket where the cold sun
Is melting. But, at last, the end is reached;
We start our cars. The preacher's mouthings still
Deafen my poor relations on the hill:
Their sunken landmarks echo what our fathers preached.

III

'Five Years Later'

This Easter, Arthur Winslow, five years gone
I came to mourn you, not to praise the craft
That netted you a million dollars, late
Hosing [25] out gold in Colarado's waste,
Then lost it all in Boston real estate.
Now from the train, at dawn
Leaving Columbus in Ohio, shell [26]
On shell of our stark culture strikes the sun
To fill my head with all our fathers won
When Cotton Mather [27] wrestled with the fiends from hell.

You must have hankered for our family's craft: [28]
The block-house Edward made, the Governor,
At Marshfield, and the slight coin-silver spoons
The Sheriff beat to shame the gaunt Revere, [29]
And General Stark's [30] course bas-relief in bronze
Set on your granite shaft
In rough Dunbarton; for what else could bring
You, Arthur, to the veined and alien West
But devil's notions that your gold at least
Could give back life to men who whipped or backed the King? [31]

[25]Hosing out gold: The reference is to a form of mining called 'placer' mining. Where gold was only lightly covered, it could be washed out by means of a high-pressure hose.

[26]Notice the echo of earlier uses of 'shell' and 'stark'. Here the first connotations of the words are suggestive of the emptiness of contemporary life. The lifelessness of the modern buildings are symbolic of an empty lifeless culture.

[27]Cotton Mather, the New England Puritan divine who fought evil so hard, is here placed against the symbolic buildings in such a way as to suggest comparisons between spiritual salvation and contemporary materialism.

[28]Our family's craft: Edward Winslow was the illustrious ancestor who arrived on the *Mayflower* and was eventually made governor. There is a sly play on the word 'craft'.

[29]Paul Revere: He was the Boston post rider who carried the message of the battle of Lexington. He was also a noted engraver and silversmith.

[30]General Stark: This was John Stark, the frontiersman who was made a colonel at the Battle of Bunker Hill and later a general. Lowell traced his ancestry through his mother.

[31]Whipped or backed the King: This is a reference to those who fought on either side in the Revolutionary War. The 'devil's notions' would seem to mean the exaggerated wish for gold as though it could confer immortality.

IV

'A Prayer for My Grandfather to our Lady'[32]

Mother, for these three hundred years or more
Neither our clippers nor our slavers reached
The haven of your peace in this Bay State:
Neither my father nor his father. Beached
On these dry flats of fishy real estate,
O Mother, I implore
Your scorched, blue thunderbreasts of love to pour
Buckets of blessings on my burning head
Until I rise like Lazarus from the dead:[33]
Lavabis nos et super nivem dealbabor[34]

"On Copley Square,[35] I saw you hold the door
To Trinity[36] the costly Church, and saw
The painted Paradise of harps and lutes
Sink like Atlantis in the Devil's jaw
And knock the Devil's teeth out by the roots;
But when I strike for shore
I find no painted idols to adore:
Hell is burned out, heaven's harp-strings are slack.
Mother, run to the chalice, and bring back
Blood on your finger-tips for Lazarus who was poor."[37]

(First collected in *Lord Weary's Castle* (1946). Reprinted in *Poems 1938–1949*
pp 29–32.)

Discussion

3.3 The first and most obvious fact relating to the form of this poem is that it consists of four separate sections, each made up of two ten-line stanzas. The immediate effect of this separation is to give the impression of four distinct areas of thought. This is emphasized by the differences in time and space underlined by the four sub-titles. The setting for part one is a private section of Massachusetts Hospital shortly after Easter. In the second part the scene is Dunbarton, New Hampshire at the family cemetery when Arthur Winslow is buried. The third part is headed 'Five Years Later' and appears not to have a defined location although reference is made to a train journey from Columbus a town in Ohio. The last part appears to move out of the mortal world of time and space in the form of a prayer on behalf of Arthur Winslow.

---

[32]A Prayer for My Grandfather to Our Lady: Note the echo here of Villon's 'Ballade pur prier Nostre Dame'. There is also a literal translation of a line from this poem in Lowell's

 The painted Paradise of harps and lutes.

Here are the relevant lines from Villon.

 Au moustier voi dont suis paroissienne
 Paradis peint, où sont harpes et lus,
 Et un enfer où damnez sont boullus.

[33]Lazarus from the dead: See John 11: 11–43.

[34]*Lavabis nos et super nivem dealbabor*: 'You shall wash us and I shall be made whiter than snow.'

[35]Copley Square: A square which in days of old Boston would be a very prestigious address.

[36]Trinity: A Church to which the residents of Copley Square would normally go to worship and/or be seen. The 'costly' is double-edged.

[37]Lazarus who was poor: See Luke 16: 19–31. This is the parable of the wealthy man who was sent to hell and asked that the beggar Lazarus be allowed to dip his finger in cold water to cool his tongue.

3.4 A further rather obvious feature of this poem is a regularity of metre and rhyme. The immediate effect of this regularity is to give the impression of formality. It is this which helps produce the elegiac note. The basic pattern of each stanza is a very regular iambic pentameter varied at line six with a trimeter and line ten with a hexameter (or alexandrine). The regular, if intricate, rhyme scheme complements the metre's tendency to formality by giving a suggestion of finality to the lines so that many of them have the appearance of statements despite the fact that syntax and punctuation require no pause. See for example stanza one of 'Dunbarton'.

> The stones are yellow and grass is gray
> Past Concord by the rotten lake and hill
> Where crutch and trumpet meet the limousine
> And half-forgotten Starks and Winslows fill
> The granite plot and the dwarf pines are green
> From watching for the day
> When the great year of the little yeomen come
> Bringing its landed Promise and the faith
> That made the Pilgrim Makers take a lathe
> And point their wooden steeples lest the Word be dumb.

3.5 The sense of inevitability induced by this strong rhyme scheme when matched by the iambic pentameter invests the lines with a solemnity which encompasses the visual image of ailing relatives waiting at the cemetery with 'crutch and trumpet'. The last line of each stanza with its extra foot has the same effect of formal conclusion. Indeed, the practice of ending a stanza on an alexandrine for that very reason, is traditional and can be seen in the work of say, Spenser and Dryden.

3.6 The note of solemnity is maintained despite a choice of words which, occasionally, seem to work against it. See for example stanza two in part one. In this description of the Sunday scene in the Public Gardens the periphrasis only just avoids the comic.

> . . . where
> The bread-stuffed ducks are brooding, where with tub
> And strainer the mid-Sunday Irish scare
> The sun-struck shallows for the dusky chub
> This Easter. . .

There is a similar tension between the form and the words chosen in the image of Winslow wrestling with the crab cancer and in the prayer of the last part where Winslow is made to

> . . . implore
> Your scorched, blue thunderbreasts of love to pour
> *Buckets* of blessings on my burning head.
> (My italics)

What are we to make of these discrepancies where the overall note of solemnity seems threatened? My first suggestion is that we should give Lowell the benefit of the doubt and assume that he knew very well what he was doing. My second suggestion is that we look for the answer in Lowell's treatment of the past.

3.7 The past in this poem is the past of New England Puritanism, of Cotton Mather and the 'Pilgrim Makers'. That is to say, it is the past of family history, of Edward (Governor) Winslow, of General Stark and other 'poor relations on the hill' in Dunbarton. Grandfather Winslow and the participating narrator of the poem are alike in that they are members of the same family and therefore share its heritage. They are, however, fundamentally dissimilar in the fact that they relate to different periods of time.

3.8 From the perspective of the vividly realized present, the participating narrator has no difficulty in placing his grandfather's materialism in a proper moral context. The essential triviality of gold hunting in Colorado and land speculations in Boston is made clear, first against the background of the earlier Puritans and overall against the constant fact of mortality. That is to say, the emptiness of examples of twentieth-century culture is seen beside Cotton Mather's spiritual struggles:

> Leaving Columbus in Ohio, shell
> On shell of our stark culture strikes the sun
> To fill my head with all our fathers won
> When Cotton Mather wrestled with the fiends from hell.

And Winslow's reported belief in

> . . . Devil's notions that your gold at least
> Could give back life to men who whipped or backed the King.

is, after all, part of a memorial poem – this alone testifies to the falsity of such notions.

3.9 However, this moral placing of Grandfather Winslow's materialism should not be thought to be done in order to elevate the 'Pilgrim Makers'. The perspective of the present also allows the narrator to place *their* preoccupations in context. Notice how in 'Dunbarton', through an image of sounds not heard, a criticism is advanced: a criticism not less effective for being phrased with comic ambiguity.

> . . . The preacher's mouthings still
> Deafen my poor relations on the hill:
> Their sunken landmarks echo what our fathers preached.

It seems that even in death religious 'mouthings' *still* (a nice play on this word) assail the ears to the exclusion of all else. The idea is contained and extended in the notion of the religious texts carved on the tombstones, those 'sunken landmarks', *echoing* the religious exhortations.

3.10 The intellectual position of the narrator of this poem seems to be an awareness of the shortcomings of his New England family. It is this fact which might have made it impossible to write an elegy which is, by definition, a song of lamentation. However, neither the recent past, in the form of his grandfather, not the more remote past, in the form of the seventeenth-century Puritans, was the prime target for Lowell in this poem. The lamentation is based upon the dismissal of the preoccupations and values of those past generations, but the tone of the dismissal indicates a non-patronizing tolerance of their position. The result is the creation of a poem which, very daringly, is mock elegiac.

3.11 The continual contrast which exists between, say, Arthur Winslow's real position and the manner of expressing it, testifies to Lowell's intention. In 'Five Years Later' the conscious hint of a comparison with Shakespeare's Mark Antony and Caesar is there:[38]

---

[38]See *Julius Caesar* III. ii. 79 'I come to bury Caesar not to praise him.'

> This Easter, Arthur Winslow, five years gone
> I came to mourn you, not to praise the craft
> That netted you a million dollars, late

but not as savage criticism of Arthur Winslow. Similarly, the classical allusion to the crab with which his death is related, serves not to belittle him but rather to point up the inappropriateness of classical allusion. The same is true of the Christian myth as Lowell shows when he adds it to the Greek myth to produce the comic image of Jesus walking the waves

>   . . . to run
> Arthur upon a trumpeting black swan
> Beyond Charles River to the Acheron.

The same impulse is clearly behind the expression of the 'preacher's mouthings' already quoted. It also determines the unusual choice of words such as 'squeakings' in stanza one of part one and the description of swans as 'swanboats'. It clearly is the reason for the over-dignified circumlocution for the fishing Irishmen already quoted.

3.12   The effect of the humorous acceptance of the mistaken values of the past is to open up a large question about the true position of the narrator. It is in this area that the nature of the lamentation becomes apparent. The last part of the work, the 'Prayer For My Grandfather to Our Lady', continues the stanzaic form of the rest of the poem but there are significant changes. Although there had been a slight change of rhyme scheme for the third part, in this last part it is radically altered. The very last stanza shows most change, moving from a basic *abcbcadeed* to *aababaacca*. This alone would draw attention to it but Lowell separates it from the first stanza of this last part by enclosing it in quotation marks. Since the two stanzas appear to be a prayer for the grandfather this is rather puzzling. However, there is a clue in the fact that each stanza refers to a different Lazarus. The first stanza makes reference to the story of Lazarus who was raised from the dead in John's story (John 11: 11–43), and the second stanza to the parable in Luke (Luke 16: 19–31) about the beggar who the rich man in hell wished to send to dip his finger in water to cool the rich man's tongue. Both stories are applicable to a prayer uttered by Arthur Winslow but the true nature of the lament becomes apparent when it is seen that the last stanza is also applicable to the poetic 'I'. He sees clearly the shortcomings of earlier generations but himself suffers the special agony of having nothing to believe in, neither heaven, nor hell. Neither materialism, nor Puritanism.

> But when I strike for shore
> I find no painted idols to adore:
> Hell is burned out, heaven's harp-strings are slack.

The Lazarus story is changed because the cooling finger-tip of water is changed to blood and the sufferer is now Lazarus, the beggar. The clear-sighted appreciation of the contemporary is, therefore, not such a great benefit.■

3.13   ■   The next poem I would like you to read also makes use of the Puritan heritage. It too was first collected in *Lord Weary's Castle* and then in *Poems 1938–1949*. As you read it try, once again, to relate the form to the content. Try, particularly, to decide how your awareness of the personality of the narrator of the letter/poem affects your appreciation of the details related. The following outline will give you the necessary factual background upon which Lowell bases his poem.

3.14 In 1734 in Northampton, there began a religious revival movement which spread to neighbouring towns and villages and in the course of the next fifteen years spread throughout New England and the middle colonies. The centre of this 'Great Awakening' as it came to be known was a 31 year old Puritan pastor named Jonathan Edwards. On 30 May 1735 he wrote a letter to a Boston clergyman, Benjamin Colman, apparently in answer to a request for information about the incredible mixture of terror and enthusiasm which characterized the 'Great Awakening'. This letter was later expanded with further details of the consequences of the revivalism.

After the Surprising Conversions

September twenty-second, Sir: today
I answer. In the latter part of May,
Hard on our Lord's Ascension, it began
To be more sensible.[39] A gentleman
Of more than common understanding, strict
In morals, pious in behaviour, kicked
Against our goad. A man of some renown,[40]
An useful, honoured person in the town,
He came of melancholy parents; prone
To secret spells, for years they kept alone –
His uncle, I believe, was killed of it:
Good people, but of too much or little wit.
I preached one Sabbath on a text from Kings;
He showed concernment for his soul. Some things
In his experience were hopeful. He
Would sit and watch the wind knocking a tree
And praise this countryside our Lord has made.
Once when a poor man's heifer died, he laid
A shilling on the doorsill; though a thirst
For loving shook him like a snake, he durst
Not entertain much hope of his estate
In heaven. Once we saw him sitting late
Behind his attic window by a light
That guttered on his Bible; through that night
He meditated terror, and he seemed
Beyond advice or reason, for he dreamed
That he was called to trumpet Judgment Day
To Concord. In the latter part of May
He cut his throat. And though the coroner
Judged him delirious, soon a noisome stir
Palsied our village. At Jehovah's nod
Satan seemed more let loose amongst us: God
Abandoned us to Satan, and he pressed
Us hard, until we thought we could not rest
Till we had done with life. Content was gone.
All the good work was quashed. We were undone.
The breath of God had carried out a planned
And sensible withdrawal from this land;
The multitude, once unconcerned with doubt,

---

[39]Sensible: In the eighteenth century use of the term as being perceptible to the senses.
[40]The man who committed suicide was Joseph Hawley, a leading merchant of the day married to Edwards' aunt, Rebekah.

Once neither callous, curious nor devout,
Jumped at broad noon, as though some peddler groaned
At it in its familiar twang: 'My friend,
Cut your own throat. Cut your own throat. Now! Now!'
September twenty-second, Sir, the bough
Cracks with the unpicked apples, and at dawn
The small-mouth bass breaks water, gorged with spawn.

(First collected in *Lord Weary's Castle* (1946). Reprinted in *Poems 1938–1949* p 71.)

3.15 How appropriate do you find this form for this content? Were you aware of an ironic distance between what Edwards says and what the poet's presentation suggests? Can you see how the imagery carries the overall sense?

Discussion

3.16 I would be surprised if your initial reaction is not to feel that the use of the dignified ten-syllabic line, rhyming in pairs, is well suited to the personality of this New England Puritan who narrates the story of a suicide. The formal regularity of enjambed heroic couplet combines well with occasional archaisms – 'kicked/ Against our goad', 'durst' – to suggest colloquial authenticity. However, as in the previous poem, a rather puzzling discrepancy is also apparent.

3.17 In the poem 'In Memory of Arthur Winslow' Lowell has introduced an ironic contrast between the elegiac form and the actual content in order to concentrate our attention upon the predicament of the narrator. This poem 'After the Surprising Conversions' also works through irony but here the distance is between the narrator's assessment of his story and the actual effect which his means of expressing this story produces.

3.18 Our first reaction to the harsh, unbending attitude of the narrator is to relate it to what we know of the stern morality of the New England Puritan. However, the patronizing, patrician attitude of the narrator disturbs any tendency towards a sympathy for him.

3.19 I suggest that our sense of disquiet probably comes from the way we are told of Hawley's acceptance of his position as not being one of God's elect. We hear of his generosity, of his love for God-given beauty, his strict morality and pious behaviour. Why should such a man not attain Grace? More particularly, why should he commit suicide? The answer has to do with the fact that the community lived according to the strict moral code of Calvinism which believed in man's total and innate depravity. This code also recognized the doctrine of predestination whereby one was either predestined for heaven or one was not; there was no way of earning one's election in Heaven. Edwards' expression of the story in this letter/poem indicates his total acceptance of this religious code and what the narrative manner reveals – almost as self-satire – is a cruelly unsympathetic authority which, in the name of religion, compelled unthinking conformity and punished unorthodox sensitivity.

3.20 It is worth considering the technique which suggests the deeper level of meaning and in this connection there are three key moments in the poem.

3.21 The first occurs when Lowell has Edwards relate Hawley's paradox: he was a good religious man but not in a state of Grace. This, of course was the Puritan dilemma. Lowell's imagery, however, is crucial –

> . . . though a thirst
> For loving shock him like a snake, he durst

> Not entertain much hope of his estate
> In heaven.

Here the snake image, taken in conjunction with the idea already suggested of Hawley praising 'this countryside our Lord has made', carries overtones of Adam in the Garden of Eden. The fact that the 'thirst for loving' is related to the snake simile sets the 'sin' of Hawley in an ironic perspective and shows up the short-comings of Edwards' position. Hawley's attempt to equate his own intuitions of 'hopeful' things with the Puritan doctrine of Grace is dubbed as kicking 'against our goad' and not to be tolerated. The more Hawley 'meditated terror', the more bemused he became and so was judged 'delirious'.

3.22   The second key point follows immediately and extends the imagery of Adam's Fall. Edwards' understanding of the situation in the community after Hawley cut his throat is derived from his belief in God's original punishment of Adam after the first Fall.

> At Jehovah's nod
> Satan seemed more let loose amongst us.

There is careful ambiguity in the use of the work 'nod'. In Edwards' view it would indicate that, having broken faith, Adam is exposed to the devil's torments. That would be God's punishment. However, 'nod' can imply sleep, and even if that is not its primary meaning, in the Manichean notion of a pact between God and Satan, an extremely harsh theology is suggested.

3.23   The third point at which the Fall imagery is extended continues the dual presentation by which Edwards is made to speak more truly than he knows. The poem ends with an arresting couplet which is explicable only in the terms of the duality. In a return to the decorous opening of the poem, Lowell has Edwards speak in doleful terms of the unnatural state of the countryside following this contemporary Fall. For him, the unnatural state is this:

> Sir, the bough
> Cracks with unpicked apples, and at dawn
> The small-mouth bass breaks water, gorged with spawn.

That is to say, no one is harvesting the apples and the fish are eating their own eggs. However, the deeper level of meaning which the extended image has been working to suggest is that it is the authoritarian theology which is unnatural. The duality of presentation is aptly illustrated in the reference to the 'unpicked apples' which condenses the ironic counterpointing of the 'two sins' – Hawley's and Edwards'. The last line about the fish eating its own young gives additional weight to the impression that the true explanation of the events *after* the 'Surprising Conversions' is to be found on a level other than that of the Puritan pastor.

3.24   Thus, in 'After the Surprising Conversions', we see Lowell again using the indirect method of presentation in which irony and interlocking imagery play a key role. Beneath the level of the overt moralizing of the protagonist, by the selection and presentation of its imagery in particular, the poem enacts a truth which inverts the spoken values of Edwards and reveals a statement which transcends the notions of Puritanism. Clearly, a crucial part of this method is an awareness of the personality of the 'I' of the poem. In a poem like 'After the Surprising Conversions', where a persona from the nation's past is adopted, it is relatively easy to form an opinion about the narrator. It is a different matter when the 'I' appears to be Lowell himself.

3.25 ■ In the following poem try to see if some of the characteristics so far discussed apply to an apparently personal experience.

Memories of West Street and Lepke

Only teaching on Tuesdays, book-worming
in pyjamas fresh from the washer each morning,
I hog a whole house on Boston's
'hardly passionate Marlborough Street',
where even the man
scavenging filth in the back alley trash cans,
has two children, a beach wagon, a helpmate,
and is 'a young Republican'.
I have a nine months' daughter,
young enough to be my granddaughter.
Like the sun she rises in her flame-flamingo infants' wear.

There are the tranquillized *Fifties*,
and I am forty. Ought I to regret my seedtime?
I was a fire-breathing Catholic C.O.,
and made my manic statement,
telling off the state and president, and then
sat waiting sentence in the bull pen
beside a negro boy with curlicues
of marijuana in his hair.

Given a year,
I walked on the roof of the West Street Jail, a short
enclosure like my school soccer court,
and saw the Hudson River once a day
through sooty clothesline entanglements
and bleaching khaki tenements.
Strolling, I yammered metaphysics with Abramowitz,
a jaundice-yellow ('it's really tan')
and fly-weight pacifist,
so vegetarian,
he wore rope shoes and preferred fallen fruit.
He tried to convert Bioff and Brown,
the Hollywood pimps, to his diet.
Hairy, muscular, suburban,
wearing chocolate double-breasted suits,
they blew their tops and beat him black and blue.

I was so out of things, I'd never heard
of the Jehovah's Witnesses.
'Are you a C.O.?' I asked a fellow jailbird.
'No,' he answered, 'I'm a J.W.'
He taught me the hospital 'tuck',
and pointed out the T-shirted back
of *Murder Incorporated*'s Czar Lepke,
there piling towels on a rack,
or dawdling off to his little segregated cell full
of things forbidden the common man:
a portable radio, a dresser, two toy American
flags tied together with a ribbon of Easter palm.
Flabby, bald, lobotomized,
he drifted in a sheepish calm,

        where no agonizing reappraisal[41]
        jarred his concentration on the electric chair –
        hanging like an oasis in his air
        of lost connections . . . .

    (*Life Studies* (1959).)

3.26   In this poem there are some obviously personal details. Lowell refers to his house in
        Boston where he lived while on the faculty of Boston University. He also speaks of his
        daughter and the one-year jail sentence he was given in 1943 for conscientious
        objection to the allied bombing of civilians. These kinds of personal, domestic
        details which have become an integral part of Lowell's poetry from *Life Studies*
        onwards have provoked the epithet 'confessional'. Unfortunately such a description
        implies that what is basically a method is really an end in itself. My suggestion is
        that you continue to look at the poetic 'I' of Lowell's poems in the terms already
        discussed. That is to say, to consider the possibility of an indirect presentation of the
        main burden of the poem.

3.27   Just as in 'After the Surprising Conversions' the regularity of metre and rhyme
        matches the intellectual position of the narrator, so the irregular, dislocated metre
        and arbitrary line length with occasional rhyme seem suited to the protagonist of
        'Memories of West Street and Lepke'. The opening section seems to establish a less
        than agreeable contemporary situation for him. A suggestion of a faint guilt attaching
        to 'book-worming' indolence and selfishness in hogging 'a whole house' seems to be
        present. Disillusionment with the consumer society is suggested by the picture of
        the man 'scavenging filth in the back alley trash cans' who might, or might not be
        the garbage collector. The only optimistic note in this first part comes in reference to
        the daughter but the reference comes in the ad-man's jargon of 'flame-flamingo
        infant's wear'.

3.28   The first part appears to be summed up in the second part with the description of
        'the tranquillized *Fifties*'. From this point on the poem moves into recollections of
        the narrator's past experiences in jail which came about after he made his 'manic
        statement' of conscientious objection. Since the poem opened with such an un-
        appealing description of his present circumstances, the question propounded in the
        second part – 'Ought I to regret my seedtime? – seems to be a way of asking if it
        was all worth it. And since there seems very little difference between either 'enclosures'
        or views, the question appears to be rhetorical.

3.29   In fact the terms in which the question is posed, that is to say, in the image of seed,
        growth and eventual fruition, are extremely important. A careful consideration of
        the jail experiences will indicate why.

3.30   The first 'fellow jailbird' is Abramowitz who is described as a 'pacifist' but that
        noun is considerably modified by the compound adjectives, 'jaundice-yellow' and
        'fly-weight'. How are we to understand Abramowitz? Our appreciation of his role
        in the poem is complicated by the ambiguous parenthesis, ('It's really tan'). Are
        we to imagine Abramowitz says that or the narrator? Does 'tan' mean a suntan or
        is an ethnic skin coloration suggested? In fact, the careful, concise presentation
        emphasizes a farcical ambiguity. Note how the yoking together of 'Abramowitz'/
        'pacifist', 'really tan'/'vegetarian' gives the impression of mocking humour; as does
        'metaphysics with Abramowitz'. There is also the 'joke' implicit in the man who was
        either 'jaundice-yellow' or 'tan(ned)' being beaten 'black and blue'. In addition, the
        description of Abramowitz being 'so vegetarian' that 'he wore rope shoes and

[41]'Agonizing reappraisal' is a phrase made famous by John Foster Dulles, US Secretary of State during
the Cold War and a leading Presbyterian churchman.

preferred fallen fruit' also invites laughter. The rope-soled shoes are understandable because a vegetarian might not use leather, but why 'fallen fruit' as against normal hand-picked fruit? In fact these details tell us a great deal about Abramowitz. By presenting such details in the manner outlined above, Lowell opens up doubts about the man's real principles.

3.31 You will recall that Abramowitz was beaten up because 'he tried to convert' two other inmates 'to his diet'. Although Bioff and Brown do seem to be very different from him – they are 'hairy, muscular' – it does seem an extreme reaction on their part. In fact the explanation is to be found in a realization that 'fruit' is a slang expression for a homosexual. The unifying factor of Abramowitz, Bioff and Brown is sex, albeit, relating to different 'diets'. The use of the adjective 'fallen' qualifying 'fruit' brings other ideas into the picture; ideas which widen the scope of the work by overtones of the Garden of Eden. In such a setting, images of fruit suggest flawed development from original impulses – or seedtimes. The use of such imagery is not accidental.

3.32 The last part of the poem, with its description of Lepke, the convicted assassin from *Murder Incorporated* can be seen as an indictment of a society which is flawed in its growth. Lepke can be seen as the extreme *fruit* of the capitalist ethic; murder becomes a business enterprise. Even in his condemned cell, 'Czar Lepke' is shown in relation to his attachment to the 'fruits' of the materialistic society which has nurtured his growth. His grasping of these itemized possessions is as mindless as is the young Republicans of the first part.

3.33 Seen in these terms, the first section represents the protagonist's fruition. At first glance it might seem that, although the 'manic statement' was based upon a less corrupt principle than those of his fellow inmates in jail, the result was very much like the circumstances Lepke was enduring. There might be similarity between, on the one hand, the Boston house and, on the other, the 'enclosures' such as the jail, 'the school soccer court', and Lepke's 'segregated cell'. There are, however, differences. There are no references to tokens of materialism. There is also his daughter who is presented in an image of the sun, the symbol of life and growth – subtly modified by the ad-man's jargon.

3.34 The special use of images of plant-like growth – from seed to fruit – is indicated in the way that Lowell changes a line from Villon to give him his 'Ought I to regret my seedtime?' Villon's line was 'Je plains le temps de ma jeunesse'. This is the opening line of 'Le Testament'. (See *The Penguin Book of French Verse*, p 115.) A literal translation would be: 'I regret the days of my youth.' Lowell turns it into a question and, crucially, adds the image of seedtime.

3.35 'Memories of West Street and Lepke' is, then, another poem in which Lowell has taken the indirect, that is to say the ironic way, of presenting his thoughts. In this case, as with 'After the Surprising Conversions' there is a difference between what is said on one level and what is intended on a deeper level. It is worth noting that Lowell is still able to carry out an ironic presentation even though he appears not to be using the device of a persona.■

3.36 ■ In the next poem, 'For the Union Dead', Lowell again appears to be there in person as the participating narrator. Do you feel that his use of the poetic 'I' works as well in this poem? Do you feel that the imagery is successfully integrated and interlocked and carries a large part of the meaning of the work? Further, try to relate Lowell's attitude to the past in this poem to his manner in others already discussed.

3.37 You will find the television programme *Robert Lowell* helpful at this point. Look also at the Broadcast Notes for the programme where the Pearson/Lowell discussion of *For The Union Dead* is summarized.

Figure 3   Detail from the Monument to the Union Dead (Paul Kafno)

For the Union Dead

'Relinquunt Omnia Servare Rem Publicam.'[42]

The old South Boston Aquarium stands
in a Sahara of snow now.   Its broken windows are boarded.
The bronze weathervane cod has lost half its scales.
The airy tanks are dry.

Once my nose crawled like a snail on the glass;
my hand tingled
to burst the bubbles
drifting from the noses of the cowed, compliant fish.

My hand draws back. I often sigh still
for the dark downward and vegetating kingdom
of the fish and reptile. One morning last March,
I pressed against the new barbed and galvanized

fence on the Boston Common. Behind their cage,
yellow dinosaur steamshovels were grunting
as they cropped up tons of mush and grass
to gouge their underworld garage.

Parking spaces luxuriate like civic
sandpiles in the heart of Boston.
A girdle of orange, Puritan-pumpkin coloured girders
braces the tingling Statehouse,

shaking over the excavations, as it faces Colonel Shaw
and his bell-cheeked Negro infantry
on St Gaudens' shaking Civil War relief,
propped by a plank split against the garage's earthquake.

[42]'They will leave everything to preserve the State.'

31

Two months after marching through Boston,
half the regiment was dead;
at the dedication,
William James could almost hear the bronze Negroes breathe.[43]

Their monument sticks like a fishbone
in the city's throat.
Its Colonel is as lean
as a compass-needle.

He has an angry wrenlike vigilance
a greyhound's gentle tautness;
he seems to wince at pleasure,
and suffocate for privacy.

He is out of bounds now. He rejoices in man's lovely,
peculiar power to choose life and die –
when he leads his black soldiers to death,
he cannot bend his back.

On a thousand small town New England greens,
the old white churches hold their air
of sparse, sincere rebellion; frayed flags
quilt the graveyards of the Grand Army of the Republic.

The stone statues of the abstract Union Soldier
grow slimmer and younger each year –
wasp-waisted, they doze over muskets
and muse through their sideburns . . .

Shaw's father wanted no monument
except the ditch,
where his son's body was thrown
and lost with his 'niggers.'

The ditch is nearer.
There are no statues for the last war here;
on Boyleston Street, a commercial photograph
shows Hiroshima boiling

over a Mosler Safe, the 'Rock of Ages'
that survived the blast. Space is nearer.
When I crouch to my television set,
the drained faces of Negro school-children rise like balloons.

Colonel Shaw
is riding on his bubble,
he waits
for the blesséd break.

The Aquarium is gone. Everywhere,
giant finned cars nose forward like fish;
a savage servility
slides by on grease.

(*For The Union Dead* pp 70–2.)

[43]William James: At the dedication of the monument on 31 May 1897 William James, the father of
Henry James, made a speech in which he praised the life-like quality of the monument saying that he
felt he could almost hear 'the bronze Negroes breathe'.

Figure 4   Detail from the Monument to the Union Dead (Paul Kafno)

3.38   Do you find that here Lowell evokes the real-life detail again as the basis for his metaphysical meditation? Are you aware of Lowell's ambivalant attitude to an apparently noble past? Do you feel that the imagery of fish and dedication is well integrated?

Discussion

3.39   In some ways, this, perhaps the most celebrated of Lowell's poems, is one of the most difficult. It is difficult because it is so condensed, so spare in its detail; and yet, though spare, it is extremely rich in its wide-ranging associations. Your appreciation of it will be greatly facilitated if you have, by now, begun to feel familiar with some of the themes and poetic techniques discussed earlier. In particular, if you recall the attitude to the past in, say, 'In Memory of Arthur Winslow' and the use of imagery in carrying the main burden of all the poems but especially, say, in 'After the Surprising Conversions', you will be better prepared for 'For the Union Dead'.

3.40   When writing 'In Memory of Arthur Winslow' it would have been quite possible for Lowell to have written a conventional poem of straightforward eulogy in which he placed his grandfather against a background of a noble New England past. In fact Lowell could not do this. His attitude to Arthur Winslow and the Puritan heritage prevented this. Instead, something of the notion you saw in 'Plotted' – the idea that the past gives us little room to manoeuvre in the present – helped create a different kind of elegy; an elegy for modern man in his contemporary dilemma.

3.41   When writing 'For the Union Dead' it would have been quite possible for Lowell to have written a straightforward poem of social criticism in which he placed images of an ugly present age against an heroic background of the noble past. In fact Lowell does not do that. There is indeed criticism of contemporary Boston in its urge to build parking lots –

> Parking spaces luxuriate like civic
> sandpiles in the heart of Boston . . .

but Colonel Shaw is not made to oppose this urge in any dynamic way. He seems to be still occupied with his private concerns which might or might not be the public issue of the defence of the Union.

3.42 If you look to the progression of the imagery to supply an idea of the intellectual movement of the poem, you will see that two main images dominate the work; images of fish and images of dedication.

3.43 In fact, as is usual with Lowell, all the imagery is so interlocked that it is difficult to see it individually. Thus, the closing simile of cars 'like fish' is joined by Colonel Shaw through the secondary image of bubbles. That image is itself linked to the balloon simile of the 'drained faces of Negro school-children' and also to the bubbles from the 'cowed, compliant fish' from the second stanza as well as to 'Hiroshima boiling'. The very fact of this interlocking of images carries the point that the subsuming principle is the image of memorial/dedication. How does one commemorate important issues, and, anyway, what are the important issues? This is the essence of the ironic point which Lowell is making.

3.44 The poem opens with a recollection of the recent past. The 'memorial' to that past is the wreck of the old Aquarium but chiefly it exists in the childhood memory of the bubbles which once came from the 'airy tanks'. In contemplating the St Gaudens' Civil War memorial, and the memorial of 'a thousand small town New England greens' the sensation which lingers is of a literally diminishing memorial – the flags fray, the stone statues gradually waste away. There is an ironic contrast here with the Mosler safe which appears to be indestructible – a fine monument to our present dedication to business. What is suggested by this detail is the impermanence of tangible memorials when compared to the testimony of memory. In this way the image of a bubble as the best memorial is offered, rather like the way in which the old Boston Aquarium still lives in the childhood memory, thus, Colonel Shaw is pictured as 'riding on his bubble'. The fact that society is still a long way from realizing this truth is seen in the last stanza. The fishes have gone. In their place mechanical forms move past but they are not alive, they exhale no bubbles; in the place of the 'cowed, compliant fish',

> a savage servility
> slides by on grease.

This carries overtones of ugliness and threat and the form of this last stanza extends the comment because the first line tells us that:

> The Aquarium is gone.   Everywhere . . .

That last line is a good example of the kind of effect Lowell can achieve. By placing the 'Everywhere' on the same line, even though, syntactically it is linked with the following line, the bare statement that 'the Aquarium is gone' is given a universal application. The impression is that we have all suffered the loss of the childhood event and we all appreciate the problem of trying to fix it somehow with a suitable memorial.

3.45 What Lowell achieves in this kind of poetry is a maximum of controlled association proceeding from apparently objective statements as well as the more obvious images. In that way his use of personal experience transcends the esoteric and moves to the level of general applicability.

3.46 In this poem, the personal 'I' of the narrator comes at the beginning. After stanza four, the rest of the poem (apart from the third from last stanza) avoids the personal pronoun but all the details are given as statements from the narrator. In other poems discussed earlier, Lowell uses the device of narrator within an ironic framework. In 'For the Union Dead' there is no ironic distance between the things said by the narrator and the deeper level of meaning enacted by the poem as a whole. However, the method is still the indirect one because the narrator's reflections are by no means simple statements; their allusive range is vast. ∎

3.47 In the poem which follows I hope you can see how this method is taken even further. In it most of the statements function as images and, although ostensibly a personal statement, the whole poem harnesses impressions experienced by many. I leave the analysis of this poem to you. My hope is that you will be able to apply some of the details of the early discussions to this particular work.

Waking Early Sunday Morning

O to break loose, like the chinook
salmon jumping and falling back,
nosing up to the impossible
stone and bone-crushing waterfall –
raw-jawed, weak-fleshed there, stopped by ten
steps of the roaring ladder, and then
to clear the top on the last try,
alive enough to spawn and die.

Stop, back off. The salmon breaks
water, and now my body wakes
to feel the unpolluted joy
and criminal leisure of a boy –
no rainbow smashing a dry fly
in the white run is free as I,
here squatting like a dragon on
time's hoard before the day's begun!

Vermin run for their unstopped holes;
in some dark nook a fieldmouse rolls
a marble, hours on end, then stops;
the termite in the woodwork sleeps –
listen, the creatures of the night
obsessive, casual, sure of foot,
go on grinding, while the sun's
daily remorseful blackout dawns.

Fierce, fireless mind, running downhill.
Look up and see the harbor fill:
business as usual in eclipse
goes down to the sea in ships –
wake of refuse, dacron rope,
bound for Bermuda or Good Hope,
all bright before the morning watch
the wine-dark hulls of yawl and ketch.

I watch a glass of water wet
with a fine fuzz of icy sweat,
silvery colours touched with sky,
serene in their neutrality –
yet if I shift, or change my mood,
I see some object made of wood,
background behind it of brown grain,
to darken it but not to stain.

O that the spirit could remain
tinged but untarnished by its strain!
Better dressed and stacking birch,
or lost with the Faithful at Church –
anywhere, but somewhere else!
And now the electric bells,
clearly chiming, 'Faith of our fathers,'
and now the congregation gathers.

O Bible chopped and crucified
in hymns we hear but do not read,
none of the milder subtleties
of grace or art will sweeten these
stiff quatrains shovelled out four-square –
they sing of peace, and preach despair;
yet they gave darkness some control,
and left a loophole for the soul.

No, put old clothes on, and explore
the corners of the woodshed for
its dregs and dreck: tools with no handle,
ten candle-ends not worth a candle,
old lumber banished from the Temple,
damned by Paul's precept and example,
cast from the kingdom, banned in Israel,
the wordless sign, the tinkling cymbal.

When will we see Him face to face?
Each day, He shines through darker glass.
In this small town where everything
is known, I see His vanishing
emblems, His white spire and flag-
pole sticking out above the fog,
like old white china doorknobs, sad,
slight useless things to calm the mad.

Hammering military splendour,
top-heavy Goliath in full armor –
little redemption in the mass
liquidations of their brass,
elephant and phalanx moving
with the times and still improving,
when that kingdom hit the crash:
a million foreskins stacked like trash . . .

Sing softer! But what if a new
diminuendo brings no true
tenderness, only restlessness,
excess, the hunger for success,
sanity of self-deception
fixed and kicked by reckless caution,
while we listen to the bells –
anywhere, but somewhere else!

O to break loose. All life's grandeur
is something with a girl in summer . . .
elated as the President
girdled by his establishment
this Sunday morning, free to chaff

his own thoughts with his bear-cuffed staff,
swimming nude, unbuttoned, sick
of his ghost-written rhetoric!

No weekends for the gods now. Wars
flicker, earth licks its open sores,
fresh breakage, fresh promotions, chance
assassinations, no advance.
Only man thinning out his kind
sounds through the Sabbath noon, the blind
swipe of the pruner and his knife
busy about the tree of life . . .

Pity the planet, all joy gone
from this sweet volcanic cone;
peace to our children when they fall
in small war on the heels of small
war – until the end of time
to police the earth, a ghost
orbiting forever lost
in our monotonous sublime.

(*Near the Ocean* (1967).)

4 THE CULTURAL BACKGROUND

4.1 Although my introduction to Lowell has been necessarily brief, I hope that my discussion of a representative selection of his poems will have given you some indication of his distinctive poetic charateristics. In particular, I hope that you are aware of his preference for what I have called an indirect method of presentation; that is, to have the burden of the poem carried implicitly by imagery or irony – or both – rather than by explicit statement. Further, you should also recall his frequent allusions to the past; sometimes to personal experience, or family, or national – or in a way which contains all these applications. These are some of the chief characteristics of Lowell's poetry which contribute towards the creation of his own distinctive poetic 'voice'.

4.2 There are, of course, other issues which you would need to consider in a deeper study of Lowell, and, foremost among these, is the fact of his cultural heritage. The following pages are an attempt to sketch in some of the details which will allow you to see Lowell in his American context.

4.3 It is an intriguing fact that a course on modern American poetry could most usefully have chosen the same starting point as the one we have chosen for this present course. If 1912 saw the first publication of the English anthology, *Georgian Poetry*, it also saw the first publication of a no less seminal publication in America called *Poetry: A Magazine of Verse*. The same kind of 'reshaping' urge is discernible behind the work of poets published in both magazines. Whereas the British poets were concerned to break away from 'the old Romantic and Victorian models' (see Unit 1, *English Poetry in 1912*, p 5), the American poets were breaking away from the poetic orthodoxy which was predominantly derived from a New England ethic, heavily indebted to a special Calvinistic Puritanism.

4.4 One of the most influential of the 'new' poets sponsored by the Chicagoan *Poetry* journal was, of course, Ezra Pound. He was, as a matter of fact, aged 27 in 1912. T. S. Eliot was three years younger and the two of them were the youngest as well as the most influential 'new' poets. Of the others, Vachel Lindsay was 33, Carl Sandburg 34, Robert Frost 37, and Edgar Lee Masters was 43.

4.5 Basic to the new experiments of the poets published in *Poetry* was a wish to find a new idiom by which to express a new, more authentically American ethic than that manifest in the works of New England poets of the earlier orthodoxy. The very fact that the new journal was based on Chicago and not Boston is symbolic of a shift in poetic consciousness: the movement is from New England and its Europeanized 'genteel traditions', to the West and a more native culture. It is not surprising that the new poets found inspiration in the work of Walt Whitman, for he, after 1855, had become the poet of national self-awareness. His inscription, *To Foreign Lands*, in the 1855 edition of *Leaves of Grass* speaks of his attempt 'to define America, her athletic democracy'. And the following passage from 'Democratic Vistas' (1871) spells out the explicit rejection of alien aristocratic influences. ' . . . The models of our literature, as we get it from other lands, ultramarine, have had their birth in courts, and back'd and grown in castle sunshine; all smell of princes' favours.'

4.6 The experimenting poets of the 1912 period followed Whitman's lead. Pound's poem 'A Pact' refers to the older poet's contribution in an image of woodcarving.

> It was you that broke the new wood,
> Now is a time for carving.

(Ezra Pound, *Selected Poems 1908–1959* p 45.)

The moral didacticism of, say, Longfellow, was rejected in favour of a less sentimental treatment of the American scene. Look at two short examples of the basically different approaches. The first consists of stanzas 5–7 of Longfellow's 'A Psalm of Life' (1838) and the second is a short poem from Edgar Lee Masters' *Spoon River Anthology*, published in 1915. The latter work is part of a collection of poems purporting to be epitaphs spoken by the dead of a small mid-Western town.

> In the world's broad field of battle,
>   In the bivouac of life,
> Be not like dumb, driven cattle!
>   Be a hero in the strife!
>
> Trust no Future, howe'er pleasant!
>   Let the dead Past bury its dead!
> Act, – act in the living Present!
>   Heart within, and God o'erhead!
>
> Lives of great men all remind us
>   We can make our lives sublime,
> And, departing, leave behind us
>   Footprints on the sands of time;

> I was the first fruits of the battle of Missionary Ridge.
> When I felt the bullet enter my heart
> I wished I had staid at home and gone to jail
> For stealing the hogs of Curl Trenary,
> Instead of running away and joining the army.
> Rather a thousand times the county jail

Than to lie under this marble figure with wings,
And this granite pedestal
Bearing the words, '*Pro Patria*'.[44]
What do they mean, anyway?

The moral uplift of the Longfellow piece is presented in the regular lines of the ballad form. It contrasts strongly with the harsh realism of the soldier 'hero' who joined up to avoid arrest, presented in a much freer poetic form. Instead of direct exhortation, Masters shows us the ironic gap between appearance and reality. Here is an attempt to make poetry out of real, unheroic experience, in the belief that this was the true 'wood' ready for the reshaping.

4.7 The easy polarity assumed by many poets carrying through Whitman's 'revolutionary' plans is between American vitality and European (essentially English) gentility: the former implying virility and energy, and the latter suggesting an effete and alien morality. There have been many formulations of this polarity. The most famous recent one has been Philip Rahv's 'Paleface and Redskin' dichotomy (*Image and Idea*, 1949). By this Rahv referred to the 'Paleface' who was the descendant of the New England gentility and the 'Redskin' or native-born American who spoke of the frontier or (latterly) the big cities of America.

4.8 It is interesting to consider Eliot's early work from this point of view. Think, for example, of the 'Preludes', 'Rhapsody on a Windy Night' and the shorter pieces like 'The Boston Evening Transcript' and 'Aunt Helen'. These poems are accurately objective, non-sentimental in the manner of the Masters' example rather than the Longfellow and although there is a clear criticism of the ugly aspects of early twentieth century America, it is implicit; there is no overt moralizing as would have been the case with a 'Paleface' poet.

4.9 This, however, was Eliot's early work. You might recall William Carlos Williams' description of the impact which the publication of *The Waste Land* produced on the 1912 experimenters. 'Our work staggered to a halt for a moment under the blast of Eliot's genius which gave the poem back to the academics . . . I had to watch him carry my world off with him, the fool, to the enemy.' (*Autobiography* 1952.)

4.10 Clearly, the heavy reliance upon allusions to older (and alien) cultures put Eliot nearer to the 'Paleface' camp. Pound, too, for all his 'pact' with Whitman, moved to a poetry which required a knowledge of world-wide culture rather than the strictly American experience.

4.11 This situation seems to be behind the following remarks made by Robert Lowell in his acceptance speech when presented with the National Book Award in 1960.

> Our modern poetry has a snarl on its hands. Something earth-shaking was started about fifty years ago by the generation of Eliot, Frost and William Carlos Williams. We have had a run of poetry as inspired, and perhaps as important and sadly brief as that of Baudelaire and his successors, or that of the dying Roman Republic and early Empire. Two poetries are now competing, a cooked and a raw. The cooked, marvellously expert, often seems laboriously concocted to be tasted and digested by a graduate seminar. The raw, huge blood-dripping gobbets of unseasoned experience are dished up for midnight listeners. There is a poetry that can only be studied, and a poetry that can only be declaimed, a poetry of pedantry,

[44]*Dulce et decorum est pro patria mori*: 'It is a gracious and honourable thing to die for one's country'. See also Owen's comment on this theme in Units 4–5 *Modernism and Its Origins*, p 50.

and a poetry of scandal. (Programme of the Boston Arts Festival (June 1960). 13. Quoted also by Hugh B. Staples in *Robert Lowell: The First Twenty Years* p 13.)

This, then would be the result of the two different approaches to poetry complicated by the genius of Eliot.

4.12 The need to unite the two distinct tendencies has been apparent to American poets for some time now. In a poem called 'Speaking of Poetry' (1933) John Peale Bishop makes the images of Shakespeare's Othello and Desdemona stand for the twin poles of American poetry. Othello might be royal but he was also uncivilized.

> For though Othello had his blood from kings
> his ancestry was barbarous, his ways African,
> his speech uncouth.

He appreciates delicate beauty, not for itself, but for its mystical power. Desdemona offered quite a contrast.

> Desdemona was small and fair,
> delicate as a grasshopper
> at the tag-end of summer: a Venetian
> to her noble finger tips.

And Bishop ends the poem in a way which shows how apt his images are.

> O, it is not enough
> that they should meet, naked, at dead of night
> in a small inn on a dark canal. Procurers
> less expert than Iago can arrange as much.
> The ceremony must be found
>
> Traditional, with all its symbols
> ancient as the metaphors in dreams;
> strange, with never before heard music; continuous
> until the torches deaden at the bedroom door.

Implicit in Lowell's definition of the two competing poetries is the need to find 'the ceremony' which will unite them. In fact, I would suggest that all his poetry is an attempt in this direction.

4.13 I have already suggested the basic characteristics which make up this attempt. There is, however, one further aspect which should be considered, and this also requires a backward glance towards Whitman. I refer to Whitman's notion of the role of the poet himself.

4.14 In the Preface to the 1885 edition of *Leaves of Grass*, Whitman refers to a special interpretative role for the poet.

> His spirit responds to his country's spirit . . . he incarnates its geography
> and natural life and rivers and lakes.
> . . . To him enter the essences of the real things and past and present
> events – of the enormous diversity of temperature and agriculture and
> mines – the tribes of red aborigines – the weather-beaten vessels entering
> new ports or making landings on rocky coasts . . .

4.15 The result of this rather mystical theory was the appearance in Whitman's work of a kind of generic 'I'. The notion of the representative nature of the poet, of his special way in which he somehow filters reality through his own self, had the effect of producing a total involvement of the poet within his own poetry – an immersion into the minutiae of daily experience. This was probably the main reason for Pound's early 'Quarrel' with Whitman. Pound's tendency was more towards the stance of the omniscient, detached observer.

4.16 My suggestion is that you should think of Lowell's use of the poetic 'I' in the context first suggested by Whitman, that is, as part of the attempt 'to define America'. Clearly, the influence of Eliot and the use he makes of personae, has to be taken into account too, but this context will have the merit of avoiding the wholly mis-leading notion of 'confessional poetry' and help towards a better understanding of the nature of 'the ceremony' which Lowell has attempted.

4.17 Basic to the whole 'ceremony' attempted by Lowell is the special understanding imparted by the personality of the poetic 'I'. In the presentation of the poem's personal details – in the symbols and metaphors and irony – is to be discerned an interpretative form. This is surely the most important consequence of the use of the poetic self. Although the kinds of experiences which the poet uses may appear to be humiliating, fragmentary and unpatterned – therefore confusing – in fact, the poetic form organizes these things and so there is unity. Robert Penn Warren has described this poetic effect. Speaking of the apparent confusion of ideas in much poetry, he also points out how a poem

> . . . brings to focus and embodies issues and conflicts that permeate the circumambient society with the result that the poem . . . evokes mysterious echoes in the selves of those who are drawn into it, thus providing a dialectic in the social process. The 'made thing' becomes, then, a vital emblem of the struggle toward the achieving of the self, and that mark of struggle, the human signature, is what gives the aesthetic organization its numinousness. It is what makes us feel that the 'made thing' nods mysteriously at us, at the deepest inward self. (R. Penn Warren *Democracy and Poetry*.)

The struggle of the self towards identity has long been a concern of the American writer. It now appears that this particular preoccupation is to be found in European writers and it would also seem that Lowell has his imitators. However, that his use of personal experience is not merely derived from an impulse to 'confess' should be carefully noted. Before the true significance of the apparently trivial can be revealed, a major poetic talent must be present. I hope that your first look at Lowell has been sufficient to allow you to appreciate that he is indeed a highly talented and major contemporary poet.

SUGGESTIONS FOR FURTHER READING

My first suggestion is that you should read as much of Lowell's poetry as possible. The following is an up-to-date listing of the volumes which you can expect to find very easily.

Selected Poems, Faber, 1965 (paperback)
Poems 1938–1949, Faber, 1950
Life Studies, Faber, 1959 (paperback)
Imitations, Faber, 1962 (paperback)
Phaedra, Faber, 1963
For the Union Dead, Faber, 1965
The Old Glory, Faber, 1966
Near the Ocean, Faber, 1967
The Voyage, Faber, 1968
Prometheus Bound, Faber, 1970
Notebook, Faber, 1970
For Lizzie and Harriet, Faber, 1973
History, Faber, 1973
The Dolphin, Faber, 1973

If you have been interested in particular poems discussed in this unit and would like to try more of the same before trying one of the above volumes, the following suggestions might be of use.

If you enjoyed 'Waking Early Sunday Morning' from the volume *Near the Ocean* try 'Fourth of July in Maine' and 'Central Park' from the same volume.

If you were interested in 'For the Union Dead' read 'Soft Wood' in the same volume.

If you were interested in 'Memories of West Street and Lepke' and 'Grandparents' you will probably enjoy the poems in *Life Studies*. Try 'Home after Three Months Away' and 'Beyond the Alps'.

If you liked the two early poems, 'In Memory of Arthur Winslow' and 'After the Surprising Conversions' I recommend you to read 'The Quaker Graveyard in Nantucket' and 'Mr Edwards and the Spider', both to be found in *Poems 1938–1949*.

'The Mouth of the Hudson', 'Fall, 1961' and 'Water' are reprinted in the Broadcast Notes.

A useful starting point for your own work could well be the Lowell/Seidell interview printed in the Course Reader *Twentieth Century Poetry, Critical Essays and Documents*, pp 412–22.

As for critical works on Robert Lowell, you will find a useful list in John Crick's, *Robert Lowell*, an Oliver and Boyd paperback (1974). As a sampling of Lowell criticism you would find *Critics on Robert Lowell*, edited by Jonathan Price (Allen & Unwin paperback 1971), helpful. This is also true of another collection of critical essays, edited by Thomas Parkinson under the title *Robert Lowell*. (A Spectrum Book, Prentice-Hall, 1968.)

If you would like to read a full length critical study of Robert Lowell, you might try *Pity the Masters; The Political Vision of Robert Lowell*, by Alan Williamson (Yale University Press 1974), or *The Public Poetry of Robert Lowell* by Patrick Cosgrave (Victor Gollancz Ltd 1970).

However, let me add the warning that practically all the existing critical works take a biographical line of explanation, that is, they 'explain' much of the poetry by reference to speculations about Lowell's life. In this I would urge you to follow T. S. Eliot's thought, 'Honest criticism and sensitive appreciation is directed not upon the poet but upon the poetry.'

I would like you to bear that in mind when contemplating the biographical details given in the Appendix.

SUGGESTIONS FOR FURTHER WORK

My brief introduction to Robert Lowell's poetry has concentrated upon some characteristics of his poetic manner. I have followed this line because I feel that many of the apparent difficulties are resolved when you are aware of some of his stylistic predilections. There are, of course, dangers in this approach. For one thing I risk blurring the question of poetic value. Neither 'Plotted' nor 'Outlook' can be considered as examples of Lowell at his poetic best: it is unlikely that they will ever be offered as two of his most memorable poems. On the other hand they are useful illustrations of stylistic devices; particularly the use made of the participating narrator.

However, since the knotty question of poetic quality is intimately related to the actual technique of a poem, a concentration upon the way a poem works must inevitably suggest ideas of values. The skill with which Lowell blends past and present in a special form of mock elegiac for the poem 'In Memory of Arthur Winslow' is a very important part of its excellence. Similarly, one must be aware of the carefully contrived ironic distancing of the 'I' in 'After the Surprising Conversions' and the crucial role of the imagery in 'For the Union Dead' before one can reach a full appreciation of those works. In this way I hope you have already begun to be aware of Lowell's high poetic qualities. In particular I hope you were able to appreciate the excellence of 'Waking Early Sunday Morning' which I would suggest ranks as one of the best Lowell has yet written.

1 My first suggestion, then, for further work is to read widely in Lowell's works trying to reach some appreciation of his many qualities. I think you will find it comparatively easy to do this on the level of technical competence and I would recommend you to follow that route first as it should be the most direct one to a later normative judgement. You might, for instance, like to compare Lowell's use of the poetic 'I' with Eliot's. Do you see any similarity on the grounds of ironic distancing in, say, 'Prufrock' or the 'Portrait of a Lady'? Or perhaps you feel that Yeats adopts a similar stance more frequently? Do you feel that Eliot's recommendation of poetic impersonality has any applicability to Lowell's approach to poetry? In this connection remember the passage in 'Tradition and the Individual Talent' where Eliot speaks of the artist's 'continual surrender of himself'. 'What happens is a continual surrender of himself as he is at the moment to something more valuable. The progress of an artist is a continual self-sacrifice, a continual extinction of personality.' (See the Course Reader, p 82.) Do you feel that Lowell's assimilation of the past and its realization in poetic form is an illustration of Eliot's explanation in that essay?

2 This reference to Lowell's attitude to the past brings me to another point about the nature of my discussion of Lowell's poetry. As I remarked earlier, I have deliberately avoided any suggestion that we might 'explain' his poetry by reference to his life. I am particularly hostile towards attempts to fit the poetry into phases of development which purport to match particular periods in Lowell's life. For example, his conversion to Roman Catholicism and his later disavowal of religion can be made to fit a notional pattern of 'development', as can the three marriages and the breakdowns etc., but these attempts must be wholly speculative and are ultimately unreliable. Nevertheless, at this stage in your reading you should try to understand Lowell's attitude to and treatment of such large themes as religion, the past, and modern love. Disregarding the temptations to 'explain' religion in his poetry, do you see any difference in the treatment of religion in, say, the poems you have read in *Poems 1938–1949* and, say, 'Beyond the Alps' from *Life Studies*? How does he compare with Eliot in this respect?

3 Do you in fact find very much variation in Lowell's treatment of the major issues throughout his poetry? Is there very much variation in poetic forms? If there are

any discernible changes in the form of his poetry, are they forced by an attempt to express a changing viewpoint?

4   Have you come to an appreciation of what we might call Lowell's basic position? How would you describe it? Would you agree with the following assessment which links him with Baudelaire?

> Both men have the posture of a fallen Christian. Both deal rather with the horrors of passion than the pleasures of love, and treat death as more seductive than frightening. For both of them, art emerges from profound intellection, from labour, suffering, self-disgust. They build their best poems around complex images linked by connotation, and not around arguments or events. (Irving Ehrenpreis 'The growth of a Poet' in *Critics on Robert Lowell*, ed. Jonathan Price, p 35.)

5   One obvious area for useful further study is that indicated by the term 'confessional poetry'. My own discussions of the use of the poetic 'I' in the few poems printed in the unit and my suggestions about Lowell's place in an American cultural tradition should have made clear how I feel about the word 'confessional'. How do you view it in regard to Lowell's poetry? In the discussion of poets in the units that follow you might perhaps find some applicability. Do you find it a particularly useful term when comparing, say, Sylvia Plath's work with Lowell's? Do you find they have much in common? Do they treat apparently personal experiences in similar fashions with the same intentions? How about Philip Larkin's treatment of personal details?

6   Perhaps almost as obviously the use made of allusion is worthy of your further study. In the Introduction, I noted a Miltonic reference and you will remember, among other things, references to lines from Vaughan and Villon. How does Lowell manage such allusions? Are they fully integrated into the poem? Do such details appear in the same manner in Eliot's work? In Pound's? In any other poet's work? Almost in the same vein are the references to events, places or individuals from a foreign culture. How are these esoteric references allowable in a poem?

7   In much of Lowell's poetry, particularly his latest, he seems to paint an ugly picture of modern life. Part of the force of his expression seems to come from his ability to present vivid physical detail but even more stems from the way that the physical fact becomes an image which assumes an interpretative quality. Thus, in the last stanzas of 'Skunk Hour' (*Life Studies* p 103) an apparently distasteful scene is made to embody a modified optimism.

> One dark night,
> my Tudor Ford climbed the hill's skull;
> I watched for love-cars. Lights turned down,
> they lay together, hull to hull,
> where the graveyard shelves on the town . . .
> My mind's not right.
>
> A car radio bleats,
> 'Love, O careless Love . . . ' I hear
> my ill-spirit sob in each blood cell,
> as if my hand were at its throat . . .
> I myself am hell;
> nobody's here —
>
> only skunks, that search
> in the moonlight for a bite to eat.

They march on their soles up Main Street:
white stripes, moonstruck eyes' red fire
under the chalk-dry and spar spire
of the Trinitarian Church.

I stand on top
of our back steps and breathe the rich air —
a mother skunk with her column of kittens swills the garbage pail.
She jabs her wedgehead in a cup
of sour cream, drops her ostrich tail,
and will not scare.

Here there is a Prufrock-like alienation and a description of a lifeless, loveless situation – notice that the cars seem to be the lovers – which is hellish. (See *Paradise Lost* Book IV line 75 'Which way I fly is Hell; myself am Hell.') However, there seems to be a similarity in the situations of both narrator and skunk. Apparently, one *can* live through hell. You might feel a similarity between this resolution and that in 'Memories of West Street and Lepke'. Thus, even if civilization is producing a wasteland of garbage of one kind or another, it is possible to exist within it.

Do you agree with this reading of the two poems referred to above? Can you extend the study of Lowell's exploration of the present world and find a similar resolution and similar method of expression? Do you find the same optimistic resolution in the early poetry, or is the disgust more obvious?

8   Finally, I wonder if you feel that the illustration on the front cover of this unit is apt? If I tell you it is of a chinook salmon, perhaps you will see the point. For me, so many of Lowell's fine poetic qualities are present in 'Waking Early Sunday Morning' and the image of the chinook salmon in the first stanza captures an important part of Lowell's way of looking at the world. As you read, and, I hope, re-read the poem, recall 'Plotted' and, perhaps 'Beyond the Alps'. Do you see the connections? How free is the salmon? How free is anyone? What does history tell us about human aspirations, whether noble or ignoble? If, as in 'Beyond the Alps', there seems to be little practical difference, how should the individual continue? Your appreciation of Lowell's resolution should form a good basis for a comparison with Eliot's religious resolution.

I leave you with the last stanza from 'Waking Early Sunday Morning'.

Pity the planet, all joy gone
from this sweet volcanic cone;
peace to our children when they fall
in small war on the heels of small
war — until the end of time
to police the earth, a ghost
orbiting forever lost
in our monotonous sublime.

APPENDIX   BIOGRAPHICAL DETAILS

1917   Robert Lowell was born on 1 March, in Boston, Massachusetts. He was the only child of Commander R. T. S. Lowell, US Navy, and Charlotte Winslow. Both parents were descended from famous New England Colonial families. His Great-great-uncle was James Russell Lowell, the distinguished Harvard Professor and poet, and he is a distant cousin of Amy Lowell who was such an enthusiastic convert to Imagism that Pound renamed the movement Amygism. Through his mother Lowell can trace relationship with Edward Winslow who arrived in America on the *Mayflower* and was three times elected governor of Plymouth Colony and also General John Stark, a famous soldier of the Revolution. For Lowell's attitude to his ancestors see the prose piece called '91 Revere Street' in *Life Studies* (pp 19–59).

1935–7   After study at St Marks School where he had been taught by Richard Eberhart (see *Penguin Book of Modern American Verse*, pp 229–31) he went to Harvard. His early experiments with free verse poetry and then Imagistic poems seem to have been unsatisfactory and, after spending a summer holiday with Allen Tate, he left Harvard without graduating.

1937-40 Kenyon College, majoring in Classics with John Crowe Ransom as teacher. He entered the Roman Catholic Church. Married Jean Stafford.

1940–1   After graduation from Kenyon he remained at the college to teach English literature.

1941–2   Editorial Assistant, Sheed and Ward, New York.

1942–3   Fellowship in Louisiana State University.

1943   His opposition to Allied bombing of civilians resulted in his indictment under the Selective Service Act. He was denied the status of conscientious objector (he had earlier tried unsuccessfully to enlist in the navy) and sentenced to a year and a day in a Federal Prison. He actually served less than six months.

1944   Publication of *Land of Unlikeness*.

1946   Publication of *Lord Weary's Castle*.

THE MILLS OF THE
KAVANAUGHS

ROBERT LOWELL

HARCOURT, BRACE & WORLD, INC. : NEW YORK

Figure 5   Title page of The Mills of the Kavanaughs, *1951, with drawing by Francis Parker* (Reproduced by courtesy of the publishers Harcourt Brace Jovanovich)

1947   He was awarded the Pulitzer Prize for *Lord Weary's Castle*; the American Academy of Arts and Letters Prize.

1947–8 Appointed Consultant in Poetry at the Library of Congress, Washington. He and Jean Stafford were divorced.

1949   Lowell and Elizabeth Hardwick were married.

1950   British publication of *Poems 1938–1949*, by Faber.

1951   Publication of *The Mills of the Kavanaughs*.

1959   Publication of *Life Studies* which won a National Book Award. He received a National Book Award 'for the most distinguished poetry of the previous year'. Also awarded a Ford Foundation fellowship for a study of the opera.

1961   Publication of *Imitations, Phaedra and Figaro*.

1962   Awarded the Bollingen Translation Prize.

1964–5 Publication of *For the Union Dead*. After the production of 'My Kinsman, Major Molineux' and 'Benito Cereno', directed by Jonathan Miller, the volume of plays called *The Old Glory* later won the Obie Award as the Best off-Broadway Play for 1964–5.

1967   Publication of *Near the Ocean*. Production of *Prometheus Bound*.

1968   Publication of *The Voyage*, Lowell's translations of Baudelaire from *Imitations*, with illustrations by Sidney Nolan.

1969-70 Publication of *Prometheus Bound*. Publication of *Notebook* titled *Notebook 1967–68*. This was followed by a second edition with revisions and later a revised and expanded edition.

1973   Publication of *For Lizzie and Harriet*, a reordering of some poems from *Notebook*. Publication of *History*, 80 new poems and many from *Notebook* reordered and changed. Divorced from Elizabeth Hardwick and married to Caroline Blackwood. Publication of *The Dolphin*.

REFERENCES

Crick, John (1974) *Robert Lowell*, Oliver and Boyd.

Martin, Graham and Furbank, P. N. (eds) (1975) *Twentieth Century Poetry: Critical Essays and Documents*, The Open University Press. (Course Reader)

Pound, Ezra (1975) *Selected Poems 1908–1959*, Faber. (Set book)

Price, Jonathan (1974) *Critics on Robert Lowell*, Allen and Unwin.

Rahv, Philip (1949) *Image and Idea*, New Directions.

Staples, Hugh B. (1962) *Robert Lowell: The First Twenty Years*, Faber.

Warren, R. Penn (1976) *Democracy and Poetry*, Harvard University Press.

Williams, William Carlos (1952) *Autobiography*, Random House.

ACKNOWLEDGEMENTS

I would like to thank my colleagues G. Martin, P. N. Furbank and J. Ferguson for their help and advice.

Grateful acknowledgement is also made to Faber and Faber for permission to reprint poems by Robert Lowell from *Poems 1938–1949* (1950), *Life Studies* (1959), *Near the Ocean* (1967), *For the Union Dead* (1970), *The Dolphin* (1973) and *History* (1973), and to Charles Scribner's Sons for John Peale Bishop, 'Speaking of Poetry' from *Now with his Love*, copyright 1933 Charles Scribner's Sons.